# Pittsburgh Characters

## Told by
## Pittsburgh Characters

Roy McHugh

Adrian McCoy

Abby Mendelson

Vince Leonard

Paul Maryniak

Jack Graphic

K. C. Constantine

*Edited by*
J. C. Grochot, Sr.

*Cover design by*
Lisa A. Freidhof

The ICON

D1457267

PITTSBURGH CHARACTERS
TOLD BY PITTSBURGH CHARACTERS

ISBN 1–878783–00–9

Library of Congress Catalog Card Number 90–61417

Printed in U.S.A.

# Dedication

The creators of *Pittsburgh Characters* dedicate this project to all persons who judge a city by the height and breadth of its skyline, by the flavor of its cuisine, by the glamour of its social doings, and by the razz-ma-tazz of its nightlife—this is for them, a little hint of what they're missing.

# Introduction

Several out-of-town writers have drawn comparisons between Pittsburgh and San Francisco. A few—when the topic rolled around to personality rather than scenery—dropped the idle chatter about similarities and pointed out the glaring contrasts. The iron city, one said, was blessed with the presence of many raffish characters, while the city by the bay, like other popular places to visit, was cursed with an abundance of freaks. In the aftermath of such perceptive musings, thousands of discerning tourists, wondering where to go next, invariably flocked to the hilly terrain about which dreamy songs have been composed, to the epicenter of earthquakes where little cable cars impart a more romantic notion than trolleys.

It is left to Pittsburghers, then, to savor the human qualities of their community. This book is an attempt at sharing, among appreciative natives and among contented transplants, some of the juicy tidbits, secrets, surprises, laughs, sorrows, embarrassments, shames, triumphs, motives, and antics of a handful of genuine characters—reprehensible characters, holy characters, and characters in-between—who have made their homes at the confluence of three rivers in southwestern Pennsylvania.

There was absolutely no agonizing by the local writers over which persons profiled in *Pittsburgh Characters* were the most noteworthy. There was no systematic selection process, no process of elimination, no value decision about which person *must* be put in, which *should* get dealt out, which deserved attention, and which for sure did not. The assignment was liberal and broad for these pros: think of somebody exceptionally interesting, somebody who sticks in your mind out of all the men and women you've written about, or haven't yet written about, and write only as many words as necessary to tell a story worth remembering. It was as simple as that, and there is certain to be a critic who will say, "*That* was a simple idea."

Regardless, the home-grown wordsmiths went to work—and without much expectation of financial reward. Each was paid a couple hundred bucks in case the book bombed, meaning no royalties to split. The whole project from the standpoint of the writers was funded almost entirely with sweat equity.

What nit-wit characters they must be, a young urban professional pragmatist might be tempted to spout, and then, snort (snort being used in the context of making a condescending noise, like a cluck).

Well, the writers are characters, talented characters devoted to their craft who jumped at the chance to gamble on this deal. It was a rare chance to express themselves freely—to write about something they wanted to write about, and to write without a miserly overseer gawking down onto the keyboard, waiting for them to finish, complaining that there was not enough newshole for what they wanted to say. "What the hell are you reporting, the Second Coming?" a column-inch-conscious editor on the copydesk at their old haunts probably would have screamed. "There's only so much white space between the ads, and we have to save some of it for the Bridge scores." And then, with a pencil designed for major surgery, the knuckle-head would have proceeded to carve the guts from their masterpiece.

Despite this book's obvious potential for a local writer to become instantly wealthy, internationally famous, and perhaps immortal, there were those who passed up the golden opportunity. One demanded double-digit payment by the hour, a tall order even for Random House.

Needless to say, she talked herself right out of the job. Another writer, a newspaper columnist with a gift for producing good-natured ridicule, declined because he didn't know any Pittsburgh characters. "I've been confined to the office too many years to know *anybody*," he confessed. "All they let me do is read the papers and pretend I roam the streets."

A bunch of others—who have departed the news trade for greener pastures in public relations—said they'd forgotten how to write nonfiction after being in the advertising business. Factual yarns weren't a part of their repertoires anymore, they lamented.

And then there were two who got all hyped up about the book—they were among the first to sign contracts, to cash their royalty advance checks, and to yak-yak-yak endlessly about their topics.

But they never wrote a damn thing.

Which leaves us with the lineup on the pages that follow—not benchwarmers by any means, but the best of the lot, not only in terms of how well they play, but in terms too of how much they love the game. Aside from an admirable writing style, each has an exemplary personal style—dependable, disciplined, spirited, trustworthy, humble, and sort of noble in a way that isn't the least bit icky. They are idealists and realists. Enough!

First, there is Roy McHugh, who migrated ages ago to Pittsburgh from the cornfields of the Midwest. During one of his first evenings in the sports department at the *Press*, Roy was approached by a bald, emaciated fellow carrying a shopping bag dribbling blood out the bottom. He shook hands with Roy and welcomed the new kid to the Bigtime. It was the assistant night editor, returning from the Strip District with fresh meat sold to him out the side door of a delivery truck. Roy glanced across the room to see if anybody else was getting sick, but there was just one other employee in the joint—the night editor, who was slumped over his desk from having had too many shots and beers.

Next, there is Vince Leonard, who must have interviewed every show-biz celebrity in the Twentieth Century during his career at the *Post-Gazette*. For this occasion, he chose to feature three commoners whose adventures and intellects he deemed more pithy.

There is Paul Maryniak, who covered criminal courts for the *Press* and hardly ever was allowed to inform the public about *all* it was entitled to know. Much of his material was judged by superiors to be far too shocking or offensive to print in a family newspaper. Imagine the frustrations in the daily dilemma Maryniak confronted—to report the worst of life's gruesome brutalities accurately, yet tastefully. Fortunately, he kept his notes.

There is Adrian McCoy, who focuses on lesser-known and unknown musicians, instrumentalists who never got a break, never got their names in lights, but carried on as if they had. Opportunity never knocked for them, but they answered the door anyway. You can't buy a ticket to hear them. You have to explore the back rooms and alleys. Their stage is wherever they're standing at the moment.

There is Abby Mendelson, who pieced together a classic collection of blue-collar artists. They have no entourage, no high-society benefactors. They work largely in obscurity, realizing that Pittsburgh has lunged into the future often at the expense of its past. They watch as the industrial landscape is plowed under, as neighborhoods wither. They know they cannot stop time, but they can preserve it, recast it. They shake their heads and shrug when questioned about what they think of what they're doing. They merely are telling what Pittsburgh was, what it is, and what it might become, that's all.

There is Jack Graphic, a nickname the cops gave to a 1970s police beat reporter who recently took the old Royal manual type-writer out of mothballs to rekindle a story that didn't make it past the city editor twenty years ago. Nobody back then believed the story, and had they believed it, they wouldn't have tolerated it. "Things like this don't happen," the boss snapped as he tossed the tale into the roundfile. The cops pinned the Jack Graphic moniker on the reporter because his nosiness reminded them of a make-believe reporter by that name in the Dick Tracy comic strip. The make-believe Jack Graphic, who was writing about the escapades of the cartoon detective, was *not* experiencing rejection by the make-believe editor in the funny papers. Weird, eh?

Finally, there is K. C. Constantine, the pen name for a local mystery novelist whose work has been translated into five languages, whose work has been reviewed favorably world-wide, whose work has been acclaimed by the Mystery Writers of America, whose plots and characters have been optioned by movie producers, but whose work is the best kept secret from Pittsburghers—they have to hunt pretty hard to find any of his nine novels. Yet all the stories are set in an outlying Pittsburgh town called Rocksburg, which strikingly resembles McKees Rocks at times and Greensburg at times. The hero of all the books is a down-to-earth, introspective, sensitive, uncommonly normal chief of police, Mario Balzic, who is not so much running around shooting bad guys and solving crimes as he is solving problems—universal problems caused by bureaucrats, or by big fish in little ponds, or by numbskulls who think they're smart, or by sophisticated pillars of society trying to dominate or deceive folks beneath them. Which explains the planetary appeal of K. C. Constantine. The explanation for his lack of exposure in the very place he writes from and writes about sounds too stupid to be true. It will not be discussed here, except to say that it has everything to do with chain retailers blindly taking inventory shipments of books from remote corporate decision-makers who have no interest in good books because they are good, only because the flashy ones will sell quickly in mass quantities.

Constantine has won the praise of the literary circuit, but has exerted lots of effort to shun the reputation of being literary. Literary to K. C. Constantine is an insult. Constantine is a master of simplicity in communication, a guardian of plain and proper English, choosing each word with precision so that its meaning cannot be misconstrued—so that the story has the undivided attention of the reader, so that the reader is not distracted by the teller. This is an obsession with Constantine, which is one reason nobody is supposed to know who Constantine really is.

Constantine, as his thousands of fans will attest, has respect for human dignity; sympathy for the oppressed, for the abused, and for the underprivileged—plus a hunger for understanding why people do the things they do. Until now, that is all Constantine wanted you to know about Constantine.

The cover of *Pittsburgh Characters* promised a Preface by K. C. Constantine. It is about time for that.

—J. C. G., Ed.

# Preface

## By K. C. Constantine

One of the reasons education's in such a sorry state in America is that the ruling class wants to have it both ways: they want an army of grunts smart enough to do the complicated work but not smart enough to understand the swindle. So we're barraged with stats and theories about why Johnnie can't read or write and why— the horror!—we can't compete with the Japanese. This leads to the hilarious spectacle of the chairman of Chrysler Corporation in a TV ad telling some of his higher-paid syco- phants that Chrysler cars are too better than the ones the Japanese make, all the while trying to make couchoids believe that Chrysler is in mortal competition with the Japanese and has never imported a Mitsubishi in its corporate life, so help it, cross the chairman's heart and swear on the Statue of Liberty. And that plant out in Illinois? The one where Chrysler has been making cars with those people from somewhere west of Hawaii? Well, when you're watching that commercial, just act as though that plant doesn't exist, otherwise you're going to get real confused.

The ruling class is good at this game. Not only do they keep the grunts all roiled up arguing about AIDS, drugs, race, gender, abortion, gun control, and whether the football 49ers of the 1980s are *really* better than the football Steelers of the '70s, they also harp constantly about the cost of labor in America, the terrible rate of productivity here, and the general inferiority of the stuff made here. Not only is their collective thumb on that scale, then they try to make people feel guilty for going on unemployment when the plants mysteriously have no more orders. And then, of course, when the grunts run out of unemployment, the ruling class commits the ultimate indignity. They stop counting the grunts. First, they put them out of work because they cost too much and they're incompetent because they're not educated enough, then they say unemployment insurance is something for nothing, and then they say the grunts don't even live here anymore.

This leads to the even more hilarious spectacle of a bureaucrat from the state Bureau of Employment Security saying with a cheery grin that unemployment in a certain county is back under 5.5 percent, while Welfare Department bureaucrats in that same county simply will not tell you how many people are on welfare in that same county. If you press them about it, they want to know who you are and why you want to know this. You tell them you're not asking for the location of ICBM silos, all you want to know is how come there are all these people on welfare if unemployment is so low. They put you on hold. Then they transfer your call to some other bureaucrat who asks the same questions and puts you on hold even longer. Then finally you get the number of the home office of the Welfare Department in Harrisburg and then you really find out what the telephone tango sounds like. Everybody who picks up the phone wants to know who you are and why you want this information, exactly. Your answer that you are a citizen and you want to know what's happening to some of your tax dollars is not good enough. Finally, you get passed to the man himself, the di-rec-tor of the bureau, the big boss man his ownself. Except he's not in. So you get to answer the same questions all over again for his secretary. And she, of course, is not at liberty to divulge the information you want. So she takes your name and promises to pass your request along, and a month later when you call back, well of course she has given the big boss man your request, do you think she would fib about something like that? No, she doesn't know why he hasn't gotten back to you, but she's sure there's a reason. Hold on; she'll ask him. And when she comes back on to tell you, she says that the reason the BBM has not gotten back to you is because— ta ta!—he's still thinking about it.

Oh.

So the grunts still live here, so to speak, they just don't work here. Well, a lot of them don't live here anymore either. Census bureaucrats put their hands up in the back of the room after all the public relationoids stopped cheering about how Pittsburgh was just the peachiest place in the whole galaxy to be living in, and the censuscrats said in a voice so low you could hardly hear, well, sure it's a great place, we mean we live here and we wouldn't move for anything, but, uh, our numbers show a hundred thousand people moved away since the last census. Our figures are preliminary, of course.

Oh.

And maybe if you can be made to swallow how uneducated you are, how much you cost, how incompetent you are, how guilty you ought to be for taking insurance money and food stamps, then maybe you can also be made to swallow that not only don't you exist, but maybe you never existed. Maybe you can be made to feel like a presumptuous shit for ever daring to believe you had any right to exist.

Not long ago, I happened to see Louis Farrakhan on the Donahue TV show. I'm not going to speak here about Farrakhan's merits, demerits, sense, or nonsense. What struck me was the reaction of a mostly white audience to Farrakhan's statements that blacks had worked here for nothing for two hundred and fifty years and that fact alone ought to be worth something in terms of reparations. The general reaction of whites (hardly members of the ruling class; they own the networks, they don't sit in the cheap seats) was that, yes, there was something called slavery, but what did *that* have to do with anything that was happening today? Farrakhan stayed cool, but some of his associates were having trouble trying to deal with this wholesale refusal to acknowledge their story.

I had the same trouble the day I tried to explain to somebody that what football Hall of Famer Jimmy Brown said on a Pittsburgh TV show was not only a lie, but a dangerous lie. Brown said that in America if you weren't descended from slaves, then you were descended from slave owners. That had a nice pithy sound to it, but it was bunk. I am descended from slaves and my ancestors' skin was the same color as their masters'. Czar Alexander II freed the slaves in Russia in 1862 one year before Lincoln wrote the Emancipation Proclamation and several years before the Thirteenth Amendment was ratified. But I don't fit the notion of what a descendant of slaves is supposed to look like in America, so therefore I must not be. But trying to explain that is not half as hard as trying to explain that I know more about how slavery actually works in America than most black people.

Truth is, any writer whose books are in public lending libraries in the U.S.A. knows plenty about involuntary servitude. Libraries buy books for 50, sometimes 60 percent discount off retail. Then they give the books away to everybody with a library card until the covers fall off, then they tape the covers on, throw the book in a pile, and sell it for a quarter. Any writer who sees that one copy of one of his books in one library has been lent twenty-six times in one year, fifty-two times in two years, and knows that he was paid only one royalty from the time the library made the original purchase knows plenty about involuntary servitude. Ask any writer if any librarian has ever asked if it was okay to give away his work, ask if he ever got a thank-you note from a librarian or from any of its customers. The next one who gets a thank-you card in America will be the first. And if you don't think that what happens in libraries in the U.S. is a theft of services on the same scale as the enslavement of blacks, consider this: the U.S.A. is the only so-called modern representative democracy which has NOT figured out some way to compensate writers for the income libraries have been taking from writers since Ben Franklin started the first one in Philadelphia. Ask any teacher in this country what *plagiarism* means and I guarantee you that the theft of words I've just described will *not* be in the definition. The library system is here. It was created by one of our founding folk heroes. It is almost synonymous with philanthropy: the words *Carnegie Library* go together like pizza and beer, but Carnegie's idea of philanthropy was as twisted as any plantation owner's. Andy Carnegie built the buildings and satisfied the longings of his Calvinistic soul, but it never once occurred to him to ask a writer how he felt about being part of that institutionalized largesse.

But this is what happens when the ruling class wants to make themselves feel warm and fuzzy. Who else could have created the tax-exempt foundation? The same people who created tax-supported libraries. They serve almost the same purpose: the ruling class can keep their money *and* give it away so they can keep more of it so they can feel good about having done their civic duty to provide books for the grunts at the same time they can complain about the hired help, how they smell like cheap aftershave and how little they plan for the future. I've been to museum balls. I've heard them. Hearing them is still not as bad as hearing the wanna-be's, the teachers who spout this vile filth, these outrageous slanders about the motivation and competence and hygiene of the grunts.

It is these teachers and schoolocrats, these edumators, who have devoted their lives to creating fresh fodder for the commercial-industrial tango. And every step of the way they lie about our stories. Every history in America is revised to the right flavor by the spin doctors and nurses, the anesthesiologists of our minds.

Perhaps there is nothing more unforgivable than that black people call white people "honkies." A white audience jeers Louis Farrakhan for trying to explain the unexplainable—how a nation could build an economy on slavery for two hundred and fifty years and how not one hundred and thirty years later another group of people can say that, yes, it happened, but so what? And now, blacks look at my white skin and the white skin of all of those who were themselves indentured servants or descended from slaves and equate us with their masters just because our skin shades happen to match. It is perhaps the ruling class's greatest gambit: that it manages to keep those on the bottom at each other's throats.

Try to talk race with a white man who has discovered that after thirty-five years in the mills his pension is gone, "diverted" by some shiny butt with an overview of the bankruptcy maze. Try to talk race with a black man who learned early on that if it weren't for the post office he would have no job at all. You will find an animosity truly scary. Every bit as scary as American autoworkers taking out their fury with baseball bats on a Japanese car. Their ignorance of the swindle is pathetic, but when they're swinging those bats, who wants to try to tell them?

So this book is just one small attempt to fill in the gaps in our stories. It's published so that all the ax-grinders and the willing fools the ruling classes incite to sanitize our stories can't jump in to get us to lie about ourselves.

Every time some fool with good intentions yammers about the separation of church and

state, another history book is going to find its
way into our schools telling us nothing at all
about the ferocity of the religious dissent that
led to the creation of Rhode Island or Con-
necticut. Every time some fool with good intentions yammers about the right of every
man to work without paying dues to a corrupt union, another history book is going to
tell us nothing in our schools about how
many heads got split trying to work less than
12 hours a day. Every time some Yuppie with
a Beamer says he loves to work 12 hours a
day, some history book is going to forget to
tell us about children wearing diapers in the
mills because they weren't allowed to leave
their jobs to urinate.

The garbage dumps have been sanitized.
They're sanitary landfills. They're supposed
to offend neither our noses nor our eyes nor
our drinking water. We've got platoons of en-
virocrats who are supposed to make sure of
nothing else. Somehow it still doesn't get
done. Our noses burn, our eyes tear, and in
some places in the U.S., even the Mexicans
couldn't drink the water.

Our history is sanitized, our news is sanitized. There are people who actually believe
Sam Donaldson is an obnoxious person because he asks "hard" questions. The only
thing Sam Donaldson knows about "hard"

questions is that if he ever asks one, he's going to have to get a real job. The Sam Donaldsons of this world get paid to sanitize the news by talking about the dumb stuff. While the Sammys of TV-land prattle on about AIDS and race and abortion—all subjects the ruling classes want the Sammys to prattle about—the ruling class has found another hole in the laws they pay to get looped so they can steal another couple hundred million. And as the late Senator Everett Dirkson used to say, "A couple hundred million here, a couple hundred million there, pretty soon you're talkin' real money!"

In 1982, the actor-president, who was handpicked by the military-industrial complex Dwight Eisenhower warned us about, who vowed to get government off our backs, made sure it slid from our backs to our shoulders to our hips, the better to get into our pants, to cover the—what is it now? $300 billion, $400 billion, $500 billion? anybody want to try for $600 billion—the Merlins of the mortgage business managed to steal before our very eyes.

That's how they do it, folks. That's the swindle. They keep you arguing about crap that isn't anybody's business but which *they* have turned into *the* public dialogue, and while they divert your eyes and pervert your emotions, they're into your pants with an endurance unprecedented in sexual-fiscal history. It's called a zipless screwing.

What follows is about some of the people who were here, what they did, what was done to them, what they did to others. Believe me, it's unsanitary as hell. It's real messy in fact. As messy as real history always is, and we should be glad somebody was taking notes.

▲

# A Patriot's Nightmare

## By Vince Leonard

Wyatt Butterfield's anger, steeping for nearly a half century, belies a gentle exterior. He's tall, slim, bespectacled, a man of 67 who says "call me Wyatt" the first time you meet him. Wyatt was aboard the cruiser USS Juneau when it was sunk by enemy torpedoes in Guadalcanal during World War II, and he sums up the episode—and his repressed hostility—this way: "We were abandoned and sacrificed, quote, unquote."

Wyatt was one of ten survivors from a crew of seven hundred forty-one. Five hundred fifty perished during the attack that calm but wicked morning, Friday the thirteenth of November, 1942, near the Solomon Islands in the South Pacific. Among those lost were five brothers named Sullivan, whose deaths led the Navy to adopt regulations limiting the number of family members on a single ship.

About one hundred twenty made it to three flimsy, doughnut-shaped life rafts.

Much of the time the sailors clung to sidelines while chest-deep in water.

Listening to Wyatt Butterfield, you wonder who the lucky ones were, the five hundred fifty who died quickly or those who fought sharks, thirst, exposure, hunger, terror, and hallucination for seven days and six nights—all the while their ranks dwindling. Until only ten were alive.

Decorated later for heroism, Butterfield, reflecting, said: "The medals are fine but I would have preferred a rowboat. . . ." Nothing can wipe out the nightmares.

"The USS Helena, which was eight hundred yards away, could have saved at least fifty but didn't. They hauled off instead to save their own ass. Their excuse was radio silence. I call that captain an SOB to this day. Chicken, and yellow, too. They left us for dead, all of us, without even checking."

The anger subsides, and fear and sorrow take over. It is fear and sorrow almost fifty years old, repetitious fear and sorrow, fresh every time.

Like the fourth day adrift when "a radioman was trying to get back after a short swim; some swam for exercise, cramped on the raft. A shark hit, took half his back. He was dead in two seconds, draped over the side of the raft. We pushed him back and watched the sharks eat. . . . "

Wyatt Butterfield breaks down here, one of five occasions during this telling. Each time he reaches for a handkerchief—and apologizes. He says he still has nightmares three times a week.

"Ensign Pitney was the last to go," Butterfield said. "It was on the sixth night. He went berserk. All of a sudden we heard a splash, then we heard a scream, and we knew what had happened.

"Some of the big bruisers aboard ship were the first to give up and die in the water. The littlest guy, W. E. Moore, had the courage of a lion, man. I'm talking about skinny, skinny, about one hundred twenty pounds.

"Nobody liked Moore aboard ship—some guys you just don't take to—but in the water he had the courage of a lion. Two times he went out to get shipmates who had left the raft. The third time out, he . . . didn't come back. . . . " Wyatt Butterfield pauses, then: "Our legs swelled up like balloons and our throats got so tight we couldn't swallow." Many drank sea water in futile attempts to slake the killer thirst. "They went bananas. They'd leave the raft saying they were going below, that the ship was down there, that they were going down for a sandwich, a cup of coffee, a shower. Hell, the sharks had a feast. Why would they leave?"

The only safe drinking water came from the few drops the men caught cupping their hands when it rained.

"We considered using our shirts, but they were full of oil from the explosion," Butterfield said. "The oil did help us some against sunburn, but some of the guys didn't have shirts at all. The sun burned them something fierce."

At night, the men nearly froze to death.

On the fifth night, a storm raged and the raft—"it looked like a laundry basket"—rode waves "that would put a roller coaster to shame." When morning came, and stillness with it, many more were gone, vanished.

Butterfield remembered that his dad often had said no Butterfields die young. "But I almost broke the streak. A close buddy of mine, George Mantrere, told me about it the next day. One night I hallucinated and told George that I saw my mother's car, a '36 Ford. I told him I was going to swim out to it and turn the heater on, warm up a bit, and then come back to the raft. He started slapping me around." It was Mantrere who recommended that Butterfield receive a Bronze Star.

On the seventh day, a Navy rescue plane approached, but pilot Larry Williamson could not land. His orders were to circle overhead until a destroyer arrived the next morning. The rescue plane dropped a life preserver containing a canteen of water and a container of meat.

It dropped fifty feet away from the raft and

drifted with the same tide as the raft, impossible to reach.

"We were desperate for that water," Butterfield said. "And who knew if the destroyer would get there by morning or that we could last another night?

"I borrowed a Bowie knife, shook hands with everybody, and went in . . .

"I could see maybe twenty feet down and three sharks were between me and the Mae West (life preserver). It was fifty feet away but seemed like fifty miles.

"For some reason, they just watched me. The farther I got from the raft and the closer I got to the life jacket, the more scared I got. I can't describe how scared.

"Finally I reached it, grabbed it, and started back. That's when the sharks came at me. I slashed with the Bowie. I stuck it in one pretty good. I had a hard time pulling it out but no way was I going to let go of that knife.

"The other two sharks jumped on the wounded one. I made it back to the raft with only a six-inch bruise along the bottom of my right foot, I think from bumping against shark skin, which is like sandpaper.

"We sipped from the canteen. You talk about good water. . . ."

When the rescue pilot saw what Butterfield went through to get the containers attached to the life preserver, he disobeyed orders, landed the aircraft, towed the raft for a while, then pulled the men into the safety of the plane.

"We all passed out immediately," Butterfield said.

"It's hard to say what got me through. I kept telling myself, 'I came this far, maybe just a little bit more will do it.'"

Nineteen years old, Gunnery Sergeant Wyatt Butterfield was reassigned to the destroyer USS O'Bannon. He still had to fight a war.

"They put me in gun turret No. 5, the same number I had aboard the Juneau.

"I remember the first No. 5, when the torpedo blew me right out of my shoes and dog tags. I thought I would drown but I managed to force the hatch open after the ship was under water.

"There were eight in that Juneau turret. Everybody was killed except me. Figure that one out.

"I never left the O'Bannon turret. I ate there and slept there. Why? Because everybody below decks on the Juneau never had a chance.

"I still see sharks in the ocean in my nightmares, slippery wet dorsals in the moonlight, cutting the surface like knives— eerie. And I hear the men scream. I'll never forget them as long as I live. I wake up and

I'm afraid to go back to sleep, afraid this time the sharks will get me. Once in a blue moon you might see a guy killed in an accident. But to see it happen twenty-four hours a day for seven days. . . . "

Butterfield changed the subject to his wonderful wife, three children, and three grandchildren. "They keep me going," since his retirement from a sales manager's job.

"I appreciate life a lot more now. I still dream I'm aboard the Juneau. I'm all alone. I keep calling to my shipmates but nobody answers."

▲

# Just Kidding

## By Roy McHugh

Luke Barnett was a liquor salesman from Braddock with a talent for being obnoxious. He put it to use selectively, either for money or his own entertainment. In the early years of the century, playing jokes on people—celebrities in particular—became a fad. It was done to amuse dinner guests, usually, and Luke Barnett excelled at this sort of thing. Until his son, Vince Barnett, mastered the trick, no one rivaled him. He was known as the King of the Ribbers. The noun "ribber," like the verb "rib," has all but disappeared from our vocabularies. To rib, as defined by Webster, means "to poke fun at; the tickling of one's rib to cause laughter." The way Luke Barnett tickled one's rib caused laughter, all right, but on the part of the tickled one it was likely to cause outrage, as when Luke tickled Leo Durocher's rib.

He was doing it just to keep his hand in. Durocher—notorious for his explosive temper, and for having said that nice guys finish last—reacted violently. There'd been a baseball game at Forbes Field that day, and the team Durocher managed, the Brooklyn Dodgers, had lost by one run to the Pirates after blowing a 7–0 lead. The Dodgers were staying at the William Penn Hotel, and Luke called Durocher's room from the lobby.

He said, "Leo, I'm from Brooklyn and I like to bet on these things. When you're going to throw a game like that, I wish you'd let me know. I like to make money, too."

Durocher said, "Listen, you jerk, who are you? If I knew who you were, I'd kill you."

And Luke said, "I'm down in the lobby. I won't leave until you get here."

Durocher, sputtering, promised to join him immediately. Between epithets and expletives, he shouted, "Tell me what you look like."

A man in the lobby who was wearing a red necktie appeared to be waiting for someone. Luke had noticed him. "I've got a red tie on," Luke said.

Two minutes later, the elevator door slid open and out raced Durocher. He made a beeline for the man in the necktie and grabbed him by the throat. As Pie Traynor told it—Traynor at the time was a broadcaster; his career with the Pirates as a player and then manager had ended a few years before—"there was hell to pay." Bystanders pulled Durocher off, and the man in the necktie spoke of preferring charges. So

Durocher had to apologize and then he went back to his room.

And Luke picked up the phone again and called him. He said, "I knew you were too yellow to come down here."

That was how Luke Barnett worked. He taught his methods to Vince and to both of his other sons, Luke, Jr. and Bill. Vince, as his father had, made a profitable vocation of ribbing. "It was always my bread and butter," he said near the end of his life. In the 1920s Vince had been a drama student at Carnegie Tech, an air-mail pilot, and an automobile salesman. "Then my dad took me in hand," Vince said. "He coached me, taught me dialects, taught me his waiter act." On the banquet circuit, Luke would impersonate a waiter, making himself a nuisance to the guest of honor, telling him, "Move your chair closer to the table, I can't get by you," taking away his plate before he was finished eating, pretending to spill soup on his sleeve (while never actually spilling a drop) and pretending to wipe it off with a napkin. Nobody knew that he was not the real thing except the practical-joke lovers who had hired him, and often there were riotous scenes.

Soon Vince was accomplished enough to stand in for Luke on occasion. Bill and Luke, Jr. were studying medicine. Luke, Jr., Vince used to say, was the most talented ribber of

the three, but it was Vince who got an offer
from Broadway and then Hollywood. A supporting actor and bit player, he appeared in
more than four hundred movies, meanwhile
performing at banquets and luncheons.

Vince's career and Luke's overlapped. People couldn't tell them apart. They were short
and bald and comical-looking, with long,
blunt noses and enormous ears. Vince had a
mustache—it was nothing much more than
stubble—and his lower lip protruded. Lenny
Litman, the former night-club owner, says
that Vince was even funnier than Luke, but
opinions differed about that. When Luke was
82, he fell and broke his hip and was forced
to retire. Six years later, in 1965, he died.
Vince was still acting at 69. He was 74 when
he died in 1977.

Offstage, in social situations, the Barnetts
were likable fellows, high-spirited but never
abrasively so. To hear Vince tell it, their victims always forgave them. "Every time I
pulled a rib, I made a friend," Vince said.
Perhaps he did. But Clark Gable took a
punch at him—and missed—during a party
at Joan Crawford's house. Roald Amundsen,
the Norwegian explorer, swung and did not
miss, landing on Vince's jaw—hard. Amundsen was in Pittsburgh attempting to raise
funds for an expedition to the North Pole.
He gave a talk at a dinner with some rich

men he envisioned as backers. The next speaker, by prearrangement, was Vince, who denounced him as a fraud. "This guy wouldn't be able to find the North Pole because he wouldn't know which way to go," Vince said, and that was as far as he got.

Occupational hazards were only to be expected. At still another Hollywood party, Vince was introduced to Dolores Del Rio as "Doctor Hofmann," a visitor from Germany. In her syndicated column for the Hearst papers, Louella Parsons reported the dialogue:

" 'I have many friends in Germany,' said Dolores politely. 'My pictures play there.' "

" 'You are mistaken,' replied the pseudo Doctor Hofmann. 'Your pictures do not play in Germany. The American producers are very good to present your pictures to be shown in America, but the German public is not so gullible.' "

Miss Del Rio's escort, whose name Louella Parsons withheld from her readers, made a serious effort to throttle Vince, but the henchmen he relied on for last-minute intervention did their job.

The elder Barnett had some narrow escapes too. He used a straight man at times to deliver a realistic looking fake punch, but nobody ever actually landed one, although Alan Ameche, the football player, assaulted him once at a Dapper Dan luncheon. He slammed Luke up against a wall. The closest Luke came to being socked was by an Irish saloonkeeper in Cleveland. To provide a few laughs for some friends, Luke had accused the bartender of short-changing him, and the owner of the place took offense. As he cocked his right hand, Luke, thinking even faster than he normally did, crossed himself. The Irish saloonkeeper froze in his tracks. "Oh, me good man!" he exclaimed, at the same time unclenching his fist.

The saloonkeeper, it developed, was a veteran of the ring. Luke once accosted Jack Dempsey and asked for an autograph addressing him as "Fritzie." Dempsey looked puzzled.

"Fritzie?"

"Yes," Luke said. "Aren't you Fritzie Zivic?"

"No, I'm Jack Dempsey."

"Oh," Luke said. "Excuse me. I thought you were a prize-fighter."

Gentleman Jim Corbett, one of Jack Dempsey's predecessors as heavyweight champion, was tempted to demonstrate his left-right-left combination on Luke, but forbore. Corbett, who had taken up acting, was in Pittsburgh with his vaudeville partner, Frank Tinney, and John R. Harris, the owner of the Harris Theaters, gave a dinner party for them at the William Penn, hiring Luke to play the insolent waiter. As Corbett started eating his salad, Luke snapped at him. "You're using the wrong fork." Corbett was using the right fork, but though "he prided himself on his perfection of manners and etiquette," to quote Robert W. Hughes in *The Pittsburgh Press,* he put it back down and picked up another one. He was Gentleman Jim, after all. "Still the wrong fork!" said Luke, raising his voice. "What's the matter? Don't you know nothing?" In the words of the newspaper story, Corbett "flushed angrily." The guests who were nearby "looked away in embarrassment."

Luke wouldn't quit. He said, "Haven't you ever eaten in a high-class place before?" Corbett was gritting his teeth. He advised Luke to make himself scarce—"if you know what's good for you." Luke said, "Oh-ho! Threaten me, will you? Get smart and I'll slap your face." Corbett pushed back his chair before checking himself. "It wouldn't have been fair for me to hit that man," he explained afterward. Away from the table, John Harris told Corbett he was being "taken over the jumps" by a pro, and Corbett, getting into the spirit of the occasion, agreed to play dumb. They returned to their places and Luke continued heckling Corbett. "If you eat with your knife," Luke warned him, "you'll have to leave." Everybody waited for Corbett to blow up. Wrote Hughes: "The atmosphere grew tense."

And still the abuse kept coming, until Tinney, Corbett's vaudeville partner, "could stand it no more." He "launched himself" at Luke and they fell to the floor, rolling around. Alerted by Harris, the house detective and two policemen burst into the room. They collared the two troublemakers and hustled them outside to a paddy wagon. Only then did Harris signal that the joke had gone far enough.

When they were on their way back to the dinner party, Tinney complimented Luke for "the finest acting job" he'd ever seen.

Lillian Russell's critique of Luke's acting is lost to history. The lavishly endowed stage beauty had just stepped into her limousine, which was parked outside the Davis Theater (long gone), when Luke jumped in after her. "Take me to St. Joseph's Hospital!" he shouted at Miss Russell's chauffeur. "My wife, she's sick! Take me to hospital!" He was using his Eastern European immigrant accent. Miss Russell tried to tell him that her limousine wasn't a taxicab. "You rich people!" Luke stormed. "My wife, she's dying in hospital, and you sit here wearing diamonds, wearing pearls!"

Miss Russell had nothing to say.

She was being ribbed at the instigation of her publisher husband, Alexander Moore. Miss Russell had boasted that as a professional actress she could not be hornswoggled by Luke. Her husband, knowing Luke for a virtuoso, had bet her $100 she was wrong. Miss Russell paid up.

Alec Moore's newspaper, the *Pittsburgh Leader,* is deservedly forgotten, but in Luke's day Moore was a personage. Other men like him, the decision makers and money makers of Pittsburgh, sought out Luke when in need of diversion. Watching him do his stuff—the more important the butt of the joke, the more delicious the humor—was the best show in town. A banquet without him, especially at the William Penn, was almost unthinkable. So when E. C. Eppley bought the William Penn for his hotel chain, announcing the change of ownership at a white-tie banquet in the William Penn's ballroom, there were people who made certain that Luke would be there. It was Eppley's big night and he wanted the affair to be successful. But here was this clumsy waiter lurching around, bumping into chairs and muttering under his breath.

Eppley beckoned to him. "What is your name?"

Beaming, Luke stuck out his hand. "Steve Kuroco, mister." "Steve Kuroco" was an alias he used. "Pleased to meet you."

"I didn't call you over here to meet you," Eppley said, ignoring Luke's hand. "I called

you over to tell you to watch yourself. Now,
do a better job or you'll be looking for a
new one."

The smile disappeared from Luke's face.
"So! You try to make me lose my job! Just
who do you think you are?"

"I'm the new owner of this hotel. Your
boss. Do you understand?"

"Well, I'm the head waiter," Luke said.
"People like you, who don't know how to be-
have, I put them out of here."

It was too much. "You're fired!" Eppley
told him, barely under control. "Do you hear
me? You're fired!"

Luke, so angry, it appeared, that he could
not express his feelings, turned around and
walked out. Within minutes, he was back at
the head of a delegation—co-conspirators
masquerading as waiters. He marched them
to Eppley's table. They had a spokesman.
"You can't fire this man," the spokesman
said. "He's the president of our local. If he
goes, we go. We will serve no more food
here tonight."

There were three hundred guests in the
room waiting to finish their dinners. Eppley
retracted the firing.

And very quickly wished that he hadn't.
Luke was reprimanding a banker ("Spill the
food on your lap, not the floor!") and wav-

ing his hands in excitement, oblivious—it seemed—to the fact that in one hand he held a pitcher of ice water.

Eppley jumped to his feet. "You! You! Get out! Union or no union, you're fired!"

"By this time the room was in turmoil," Luke wrote in his 1945 autobiography, *Between the Ribs*. Making his exit once more, he paused for a final salvo from the doorway:

"I tell all the people about the rotten food here! I tell how you give them leftovers! I tell how dirty the kitchen is!"

Eppley was "full of relief," Luke wrote, to learn that it was all just a prank.

At crowded cocktail parties, Luke would be the waiter with the drinks on the tray. Heavy-set (but not fat), he would shoulder his way through the guests, saying, "Pliz to make room. Everybody step aside." The mere fact of Luke's bulk—two hundred twenty pounds—encouraged obedience. "Wait your turn!" he would bellow at a male guest reaching for a glass. "Don't you know nothing? Ladies first!"

There were several variations of "Steve Kuroco." As "Jan Kuroco," a coal miner from Montana, Luke climbed onto the stage at a CIO convention and announced that he was running for president against John L. Lewis, "because the union needs a leader who has some guts." A few feet away, his shaggy black eyebrows an unmistakable badge of identity, Lewis sat glowering.

At other times Luke was either "Doctor" or "Professor" Kuroco. Invited to address a special-interest group, he would question the organization's motives and legitimacy. "Grafters!" he would shout. "You should all be in jail!"

Luke's Kuroco characters were Polish. Vince, when he wasn't "Doctor Hofmann," might be Eric von Hogenstrom, the renowned West German economist. Von Hogenstrom spoke at business conventions, infuriating his audience of corporate executives with unrestrained criticisms of their manufacturing and merchandising policies. "America," he would say, "iss a melting pot, und der more you melt, der less becomes shmart der brain. Vest Chermany und Chapan are outclassing you." Vince was more prophetic than he knew. Or maybe not.

Vince's first pigeon in Hollywood was Bobby Jones. The famous golfer had gone there to make instructional films. One afternoon when he was playing an exhibition match, Vince caddied for him, dressed like a bum. Sticking out of his back pocket was a bottle of muscatel. Jones didn't know who he was. The other golfer did. Faced with an easy approach shot, he set Jones up by asking him to recommend a club.

"Four iron," Jones said.

Vince, breaking in, said, "No, no, no! For this shot, you want a five iron."

The other player reminded him that Jones was the greatest golfer in the world.

Vince glared at Jones. "Okay, wise guy," Vince said, "you got your name in the paper a couple of times, you think you know it all."

The other golfer took the four iron and hit the ball over the green—on purpose.

"I'm sorry," said Jones. "The caddy was right."

Then as Jones was about to take his own second shot, Vince stepped in front of him and picked up his ball. "Before I forget, I'd like you to autograph this for my sister," he said. A man of unbelievable courtesy, Jones obliged, and the match continued. On the green, when Jones missed a putt before holing out, Vince shook his head in disgust. Instead of returning the putter to the golf bag, he snapped it in two over his knee. "This thing is no good," he said. "Get another one." Uncharacteristically, Jones was on the verge of having a fit. He thought he had seen the last of the putter he called Calamity Jane, and treasured. It was actually a replica, furnished by the prop department at Warner Brothers.

Howard Hughes, watching Vince from the gallery, turned to the director of "Scarface" and said, "We can use this guy in the picture." In "Scarface," Paul Muni played a character resembling Al Capone. Vince got the part of the mobster's illiterate stooge and from then on was in constant demand.

His fame soon exceeded his father's. In the role that Luke had perfected, Vince gave the business to Winston Churchill, who was seated beside Marion Davies at a dinner in Hollywood, his arm resting casually on the back of her chair. Vince brushed it off, hissing, "Please! We have rooms upstairs for that." Churchill's cigar almost fell from his mouth, but for once he was speechless.

When George Bernard Shaw visited Hollywood, Vince approached him as Shaw was having lunch.

"I'm Timothy Glutzspiegel, reporter for the Hollywood film paper. I've got to have an interview with you."

Shaw protested that he had been interviewed only that morning by half of the reporters in Southern California.

"But you gave them old stuff," Vince said. "I'm looking for something new. What do you think about the religious persecution in Mexico?"

Shaw said, "I didn't know there was any."

"You should keep up with current events better than that," Vince admonished him.

Recklessly taking on one of the world's fastest counterpunchers, he had left himself open.

"Young man," Shaw said, "I *make* current events."

As time went by, Vince lost a valuable tool—his anonymity. He was appearing in too many movies. Most people recognized his face. He tried disguises. He wore a toupee. Nothing seemed to help.

Finally, assisted by a makeup man, he passed himself off as a Cambodian army officer in a meeting with Air Force General Hap Arnold. A day or two later, set straight about Vince, Arnold introduced him to General George Marshall, the highest ranking officer in the U.S. military. Brazenly perched on the edge of Marshall's desk, Vince opened a humidor and helped himself to the cigars, grabbing a handful. He addressed Marshall as "Colonel." He said, "Colonel, I want you to give me a commission. My brother-in-law and me control the houses of ill repute and the slot machines all up and down the West Coast, and if you don't come through, we'll see there's a new chief of staff." As Marshall stared at him, unable to speak, Vince took out a bankroll, peeled off ten one-hundred-dollar bills, and spread them on the desk. "Now, Colonel," he said, "this is not a bribe. You found this money on the floor." Marshall's face had turned crimson. The veins in his neck were bulging. It was time to let him know he was being ribbed, Arnold could see.

After Marshall had cooled off, he began to feel devilish. An idea came to him. He sounded out his wife. Mrs. Marshall liked a joke as well as anyone. Thus it happened that Vince, posing as a vacuum-cleaner salesman, dropped in on a card party she was giving for the wives of some government officials. Reluctantly, they interrupted their game so that Vince could deliver his sales pitch. It went on for a good long while. The women, growing restless, started whispering to one another. Vince curtly ordered them to be quiet. He singled out one woman in particular. It was Eleanor Roosevelt. "You're talking too much," Vince said. When he was ready to show how the vacuum cleaner picked up dirt, he handed Mrs. Roosevelt the cord. "Here, lady," he said, "plug this in the wall."

Upon having Vince explained to her, Mrs. Roosevelt joined his fan club. Vince had pulled a rib and, as he always did, made a friend.

The Barnetts embarrassed people, but never for any length of time. They believed that "humor must always be kindly." "If it hurts," Luke wrote in *Between the Ribs*, "it isn't funny." Luke wasn't interested in "showing anyone up." Nor was Vince. Their "subjects," as they called them, were people they genuinely admired. And their humor was mostly verbal. They did not live to witness such juvenile innovations as the Gatorade bath for the winning football coach, but excesses of that nature were beneath them. To his dying day Luke denied that he ever spilled soup on people—"which only an idiot would think of as humorous." Together, the Barnetts were one of a kind. Their antics, as a rule, made no one look as foolish as they themselves did. Their thrusts were never telling and their jokes never obscene. And they were blessed with a kind of subtlety that transformed their mischief into something complex and creative—something that was probably close to art.

▲

# Liar's Poker

# By Paul Maryniak

Like scores of other suburban family men, Don Hughes seemed to be heeding the signs of an early spring when he entered the garage of his Washington County home on March 26, 1986. Don Hughes liked to tinker with the car, but this fair-weather day was his last for tinkering, his last hour of earthly anguish, the final act in a sinister charade.

Spring brought no promise to Don Hughes. Winter had settled bleakly on him and never would go away.

Contrary to appearances, Don Hughes was no ordinary middle-aged suburban family man. He was a crooked cop—and no ordinary crooked cop, either.

Don Hughes had sold his badge to Pittsburgh's longest-surviving corrupter of lawmen—a conniving deceiver who was at once grandfatherly and impish, soft-spoken and mild-mannered, yet impudent and cunning, smiling, coy, cold, and ruthless.

This professional manipulator had fouled the legal system when Don Hughes was a child—perverted the concept of justice with a "harmless" game of numbers. He chewed up police and spit them out every ten years or so, thus "buying" his freedom, renewing his "license" to operate. He made and destroyed careers, capitalized on human weaknesses, and tantalized the greedy.

Then, when they had worn out their usefulness, he watched their funerals on television from his comfortable Mount Lebanon easy chair.

Don Hughes was just another means to an end that brought untold wealth, power, and influence to Anthony Michael "Tony" Grosso.

Don Hughes was another expendable symbol of authority without dignity, no different to Tony Grosso than a cigarette is to a smoker who flicks its ashes onto the carpet.

Suspended without pay since the previous August, Hughes, a Pennsylvania State Police corporal, was due to stand trial in two months on bribery charges worth more than fifty years in prison. And only twenty-four hours from the time he went into his garage, Hughes was scheduled to be in Harrisburg for a preliminary hearing on perjury charges for lying to the same grand jury that had learned the secrets he tried so desperately, but unconvincingly, to conceal.

Like others before him, Hughes would take a few of those secrets to his grave.

Since 1982 Hughes had been a hunted man. At first, only he knew he was the quarry. Investigators from four different law enforcement agencies, including the one he had served for twenty-five years, were seeking to identify the infidel among them.

When the pursuit began, the pursuers were nearly crazed with paranoia—each agency eyeing the others suspiciously. All they knew at first was that someone in their ranks consistently betrayed them by leaking confidential information about telephone surveillance and gambling raids.

Many state cops wondered if the leak came from city vice detectives, who wondered about the staties. Both nervously eyed the office of Allegheny County District Attorney Robert E. Colville, whose prosecutors began dealing more gingerly and anxiously with the troopers and the city cops. State Attorney General LeRoy Zimmerman's assistants wondered if they could trust anyone in the DA's office, or in the state police, or in the Pittsburgh department.

The paranoia even had divided the state police force itself. Elite racket investigators suspected that the "mole" might be a plainclothes trooper assigned to local vice units from one of the barracks in Western Pennsylvania; distrust also ran rampant among different barracks.

By 1984, the mutual distrust had eased somewhat as the probe focused on the state police. Toward the end of that year, the inquiry narrowed further; it became a clinical dissection of Hughes' life—particularly his personal finances, his tawdry romance with his wife's best friend, and, most of all, his clandestine affair with the notorious fixer, Grosso.

It was Grosso himself, through a grapevine he invented years prior, who pointed the accusing finger at Hughes. Grosso, from experience, knew he could trade for his own freedom by sacrificing Hughes.

Hughes' arrest in August of 1985 satisfied his pursuers. But the 47-year-old Hughes said through his lawyer that the fight had just begun. He was not guilty, he told a judge. His lawyer, Thomas Corbett, a former assistant district attorney who became the U.S. Attorney for Western Pennsylvania in 1989, told reporters that Hughes was prepared to defend himself against the accusations levied by Grosso. Don Hughes seemed braced for the legal fight ahead.

Hughes' public posturing and protestations masked a dread. As the trial loomed closer, he authorized Corbett to begin quiet negotiations for a deal. Prosecutors gave Hughes their once-and-final offer: a two-and-a-half-year minimum term in a state penitentiary.

The negotiations were over. It was now up to Hughes. No one, not even Hughes himself, was certain that a deal would be signed, sealed, and delivered. Hughes remained torn between continuing the pronouncements of innocence and admitting disgrace.

In the garage that sunny March day, he—or someone else—closed the heavy door and switched on the car. As the engine rumbled, Hughes breathed, then breathed again, and again.

In death, he created a mystery—had he committed suicide or was he murdered to insure his silence? Was Grosso an executioner?

No matter what the answer to the first question, the only answer to the second, under any circumstances, was yes.

\* \* \*

For a career cop who had spent most of his time in vice circles and who lived not far from Pittsburgh, Hughes should have known better.

He had made a pact with a predictable devil.

As usual, the broken-English-speaking Mephistopheles in the Hughes case was round and neat and humble and cute during his many courtroom appearances over four decades. He looked exactly like Hollywood depicts a typical gangster boss.

No matter how elegant the cut of his silk suits, he habitually presented the image of a confused and barely literate immigrant arriving at Ellis Island—even though he was born and raised within walking distance of the two courthouses on Grant Street that became almost his second home during his sordid career.

His squat nose floated atop a constant thin smile of contemptuous amusement, and his bushy brows shadowed a twinkle of irony in his eyes.

His game never changed, no matter who played. He'd cat-and-mouse with the cops, then buy his way out with testimony when the heat rose to the boiling point. In the small busts, he needed only to rely on the people's tolerance of his crime—a crime so acceptable, so popular, that it eventually became a profitable bureaucracy for state government: the Daily Lottery.

In the big busts, he always was able to turn some of his pursuers into the pursued by ratting on officials who took his protection payoffs. Prosecutors much preferred the headlines of a political corruption case to the kind of case that a Tony Grosso gambling raid offered.

Always, he survived. And prospered.

Sometimes he would be put away, but never for very long. And when he came back, it was as if he had never been gone. His business thrived in his absence.

So practiced was his game that by the end of the 1970s he was a celebrity. Television stations and newspapers called upon him to share his expertise with their viewers and readers.

Don Hughes never had a shot at winning when he began playing ball with Grosso. Grosso was much better at beating the odds.

He was, after all, a much better liar.

*   *   *

Among the scoundrels who squeezed coins and dollars out of honest and nearly-honest Pittsburghers, Anthony Michael Grosso had few equals in the Twentieth Century. No other criminal in Pittsburgh generated more attention for so long; no other criminal so openly and brazenly defied the law; and no other so lusted for respect, even while he confessed to felonies.

He was Horatio Alger from the wrong side of the tracks.

But his story is one with a major contradiction. Even though a certain furtiveness was necessary for him to evolve from a downtown bookie into a region-wide gambling overlord, he could not resist the limelight. Grosso wanted the cops to leave him alone—and paid hundreds of thousands of dollars to achieve that—yet he sought recognition as a kingmaker and the attention of reporters as an expert on the complexities of placing a bet.

Grosso was born in December of 1913 to a railroad laborer who had sired six boys and two girls. He raised them all in a three-room house in the lower Hill District with no indoor plumbing.

To help make ends meet, young Tony began working while still in grammar school by selling newspapers, condoms, and numbers on the corner of Smithfield Street and Fifth Avenue in the Golden Triangle—not so golden then.

Even as a kid, he recognized a power broker when he saw one: he often bragged that the last customer on his route through several Downtown office buildings was financier Paul Mellon. Mellon, whose passion for French impressionistic paintings was exceeded only by his lust for hunting, was not interested in contraceptives or in wagering six-to-one on the three-digit closing stock market number that fueled poor and middle class Pittsburghers' dreams of quick money without work. Mellon was interested in the penny-a-copy newspapers that were heralding the opening of the Smithfield Street Bridge and the ground-breaking for the Cathedral of Learning, news items that often mentioned his family name.

But Grosso claimed that Mellon also had an interest in him, this grammar school kid whose birthplace one day would be razed to make way for the Civic Arena.

As Grosso recalled on the witness stand: "He used to ask me about my life, the environment I lived in, and the conditions of the poor people up on the Hill." Grosso could—and often would—say anything; Mellon was never called to the witness stand for corroboration.

Regardless, Grosso learned a valuable lesson in those early days of hawking newspapers, rubbers, and bet slips. "As time went on," he once recalled, "I got the feel for what you would call the easy buck."

And easy it was. He was knocking down $300 to $500 a week on numbers by the time he was a freshman in high school. Or so he would claim. Since truth was never Grosso's strong suit, it was—and remains—nearly impossible to say with any certainty how much money he earned at any time in his life. Still, there had to have been good money to be made; his five brothers were also numbers runners and together they went through much grief to keep the business all to themselves.

That grief, of course, came largely from

the law. Tony's first arrest came in 1938 and drew a $25 fine. When he was arrested five years later, the cost of breaking the law rose to a two-month term in the old County Workhouse. During that sentence, which he served with all his brothers, Grosso began learning the importance of staying on the good side of the law even while breaking it. He claimed he paid the Workhouse warden and guards to allow special visits from his wife, Angela, and their newly born daughter, and for other amenities, such as home-cooked meals.

After paying his debt to society, Grosso showed a sense of public service by joining the Army. Not surprisingly, he made sure there were boundaries to his sacrifice; he stayed stateside and served as a quartermaster throughout World War II. Lord knows what a crooked quartermaster with some ingenuity and no regard for regulations could do.

A more familiar kind of war awaited Grosso upon his return to civilian life. While he was away, his brother, Sam, the brains of the numbers operation for which Tony served as the muscle, had nurtured their business into a $5,000-a-day machine. By that time, they weren't just relying on what their bookies pulled in off the streets: the Grossos were

taking bets at restaurants, bars, and vacant
stores throughout Pittsburgh.

Tony Grosso had made enough money to
buy a club on Penn Avenue that catered to
the well-heeled. Called the Horseshoe Bar,
the nightspot brought in big-name entertainment talent and earned him a certain air of
respect as a convivial host to the social set.

But all his sociability and respect couldn't
keep the heat away. So Grosso took the lessons he learned in the Workhouse and applied them on the streets. He paid off beat
patrolmen and precinct sergeants to keep the
police at bay, developing a pad that was almost half the size of the city's law enforcement payroll.

And that put him on the road to his doc-
torate in public corruption, a lesson in how
to use cops until their usefulness had been
exhausted.

\* \* \*

Even in those early days, numbers—like
other forms of gambling—was a crime that
generated ambivalence among all but the
most moral, law-abiding members of the
community. Before Pennsylvania legisla-
tors recognized gambling as a wonderfully
painless and uncontroversial way of raising

revenue, judges, cops, and the public at large often seemed hard pressed to treat it as anything more than a nuisance.

As recently as 1984, a U.S. Justice Department survey found that Americans ranked the seriousness of a numbers bet on the same level as playing loud music in the neighborhood. Although a variety of investigations long had insisted that numbers generated millions of dollars to finance far more serious criminal ventures, gambling was a crime that drew a wink of an eye and a cynical reaction from all but the most rigid enforcers of the law.

Numbers proved an ideal public relations gimmick for any cop or elected official eyeing career advancement. Numbers runners made for easy arrests; easy arrests meant many arrests; and many arrests meant a clear indication to the general public that the community was being protected from menace.

It mattered little that the suspects returned to their normal lives as quickly as they had been scooped up. All that mattered was the illusion of a job well done.

For those who put up with the hassle and expense of arrests, the financial reward was impossible to pass up. The lowest-level operatives often were unemployed or handicapped people who could clear hundreds of dollars a week tax-free. And the work wasn't hard: runners could just answer the phone or amble to the local bar and sell bets among friends and acquaintances; otherwise legitimate small businessmen and women could offer a wagering service to their customers without ever leaving their shops.

Above the sidewalk-and-barstool level, the numbers business assumed Wall Street dimensions. Amid the higher tiers of the operations, bookies supervised banks and sub-banks with divisions of responsibility—some taking bets from the writers and runners every day; others collecting the net proceeds on a weekly basis.

The take was staggering, ranging from coins clinking in lunch bags to currency stuffed in shopping bags tossed over alley fences, or packed in envelopes passed between automobiles, or hidden in flour cans on kitchen counters.

Many of the city's newspaper delivery trucks were a cover for Grosso, and not just a few editors and reporters gave their bets to a driver before he departed for his daily stops to drop off bundles of *The Pittsburgh Press* and *Post-Gazette*—and pick up wagering slips from the vendors.

Numbers banks protected themselves against insolvency through the well-developed art of layoffs: each bank knew how much money it could afford to pay on any winning three-digit number; so when the amount bet on a number exceeded that pay-off limit, a small bank simply would pass along, or lay off, the excess wagers to a larger bank that could afford to handle a big hit.

The size of any individual bank depended on the bankers' success in recruiting runners, and the runners' success in drumming up business.

Grosso was the ultimate hustler in Western Pennsylvania when it came to numbers. His was the ultimate bank because he had so many people working for him. But he didn't get so big just by dint of his personality and energy. His ability to recruit workers was inextricably linked to his ability to get cops at every level to look the other way.

\* \* \*

The first big fish Grosso led to ruin was a showboat city flatfoot named Lawrence J. Maloney. Maloney was a plainclothesman who supplemented his salary by working as a janitor for a church in the East End—the same one where Mayor David L. Lawrence worshipped.

In 1947, Maloney—after a chat with Lawrence following a Sunday mass—began a climb through the ranks of the force. He went after bookies with a vengeance. Within a year, the number of his collars so pleased

"Hizzoner" that Maloney was put in charge of a new racket squad—and the arrests accelerated. He often resorted to ruses to catch his prey, posing as a millworker, or a butcher, so he could watch drop-off points long enough to figure out when an arrest would yield a sizeable enough haul to interest the newsies.

In no time, his squad was taking down an average of one hundred and fifty bookies a month, and it earned the nickname—"Maloney's Marauders." It didn't matter to the scribes that Maloney often would grab the same man on three or more consecutive days. The suspects got back out on the streets before the ink had dried on their arrest reports. Then, more ink was devoted to the weak-kneed treatment they were getting in the courts.

In 1949, Grosso had had it with Maloney. Grosso was shelling out protection money by the fistful to beat patrolmen, but his joints were still getting knocked off by Maloney and his marauders.

So, one night Grosso drove to the old police headquarters building where Maloney worked. Grosso waited until the gangbuster left for home.

"I decided to take things into my own hands," Grosso later said. "He must have arrested my people a hundred times a year and I couldn't take it. It was costing me too much money. So, I went up to him and I asked him, 'You want me to quit?' I told him I didn't mind taking my licks, but it seemed like he was just picking on me and ignoring some of my competitors in the business."

The two men reached a mutually profitable accommodation. The main marauder would get as much as $30,000. The gambling man got the cops off his back, plus a new source of business as well.

That new source of business came from Maloney himself, whose men began harassing Grosso's competitors. They forced bookies into Grosso's ever-growing numbers empire. "Maloney had nine collectors getting money from me. He had so much money that I don't think he knew what to do with it," Grosso said.

In 1950, Maloney began a crusade against La Cosa Nostra godfather John LaRocca's numbers dens in East Liberty, knocking off forty-eight bookie establishments in three weeks and effectively putting an end to the Mafia's direct involvement in numbers within the city limits. Grosso—who always claimed to have been an independent and never was shown to be otherwise—had gained a virtual monopoly on the numbers business in Pittsburgh. There was, though, a theory that he paid a percentage to LaRocca to keep the enterprise peaceful.

He celebrated his success in 1950 by moving into a stone colonial house on an exceptionally affluent corner of Mount Lebanon. Grosso never moved from that house, which, with its built-in swimming pool and three bedrooms, was a far cry from the Hill District hovel of boyhood. He relished the idea that he lived next to captains of commerce and industry. He often proudly pointed out to visitors the neighboring homes of some of the most successful executives of the city's major corporations. But then, Grosso himself was the chief executive officer of one of the city's biggest money-making ventures.

Grosso's largesse only tempted more public servants eager for his handouts. By the early 1950s, his protection payments were not just going to cops, but to politicians as well. U.S. District Judge Hubert I. Teitelbaum in 1984 publicly said he was convinced that most of Grosso's payments to Maloney went to the political machine of Mayor Lawrence. "I don't doubt some of the money stuck to Maloney, but I believe most of it went to the political machines in town," said Teitelbaum, who as a federal prosecutor helped lay the foundation for the feds' first attack on Grosso in 1964.

The arrangement between Grosso and Maloney worked out well for just about everyone. As Teitelbaum recalled in 1984, La-

Rocca was shut out of the city. Subsequent congressional hearings in the 1960s further pointed out that for as long as Maloney and Grosso maintained their relationship, Pittsburgh was relatively free of organized crime shootings, bombings, and retaliatory assaults by rivals.

Grosso's empire was no less an organized criminal cartel than LaRocca's. For some reason, though, Grosso was considered a "good criminal" as opposed to the reclusive and always elusive LaRocca, whose own businesses covered a wider range of even seamier activities, such as prostitution and extortion.

Some law enforcement authorities still believed that LaRocca moved his own numbers operations out of the city in return for a cut of Grosso's action. No evidence ever was produced to support this, however. Grosso himself insisted in 1985 he had never met LaRocca and maintained that he drove the Mafia boss out of the numbers racket in the same way he dealt with lesser gambling rivals—namely, by deftly using crooked cops to shut down the competitors who refused to become allies.

During his 1964 federal trial, Grosso testified he made his money by playing gin rummy—an assertion that the jury roundly dismissed when it convicted him after only a few hours of deliberation.

Then, facing as many as ten years in prison, Grosso played his trump card—tearing down the veneer that Maloney's lofty anti-crime campaigns had acquired. Grosso agreed to testify against Maloney if the feds reduced his sentence.

Thus was born a tradition that lasted into the 1980s.

The federal grand jury indictment of Maloney on charges of evading taxes on $250,000 in payoffs from Grosso stunned the city and shattered the image of a town that somehow had been protected from the Mafia by a hard-working force of dedicated police officers.

Pittsburghers learned that the same organized criminal ventures that Mafia informant Joe Valachi had testified about during televised congressional hearings in 1963 had, indeed, made Pittsburgh no place special for law-abiding folk. It didn't matter that La Cosa Nostra wasn't in charge of the numbers business in town; the man who was in charge was just as capable of turning cop into con.

Maloney never took the witness stand in his own defense. Instead, he let his lawyer raise enough reasonable doubt about the veracity of Grosso and the dozen other gamblers who testified against him that the chief marauder was acquitted. His counsel kept impressing the jury with the suggestion that

Maloney's personal wealth was just a matter of luck, that it came from his wagers at the track on "long shots and sure things."

Maloney chose his legal counsel wisely: he was represented by Teitelbaum, who only a year or so earlier as a federal prosecutor had started the case that ultimately gave Grosso his debut role as stool pigeon.

In press conferences after the verdict, Maloney thundered about his innocence and even said he would run for mayor. Instead, then-Public Safety Director David W. Craig, who later became a Commonwealth Court judge, fired Maloney.

The verdict kept Maloney out of jail, but dissuaded no one from thinking that he and his police department had been corrupted. Shortly after the acquittal, then U.S. Attorney General Nicholas Katzenbach said Maloney's trial showed that "gambling in Pittsburgh was wide open, with police protecting very large-scale operations." After Maloney died—in obscurity, but not poverty—the IRS went after his $691,000 estate, claiming the money was due Uncle Sam because the main marauder had never paid taxes on his ill-gotten gains from working with Grosso.

But a U.S. tax judge disagreed.

While ruling that Maloney indeed had become a rich man on Grosso's payoffs, the tax court said it appeared that most of the bribes probably did not go into his pocket. "Maloney," declared Judge William H. Quealy, "was merely a conduit through which funds passed to others."

Meanwhile, Grosso never had to worry about jail.

His lawyer appealed the federal gambling conviction and the case ultimately was torpedoed. Grosso had been convicted on technical charges that he failed to register with the IRS as someone who made his living by taking illegal bets. The U.S. Supreme Court ruled that such a "gambling tax" was unconstitutional because it violated an individual's Fifth Amendment right against self-incrimination. By requiring bookies to identify themselves as bookies, the justices decided, the government in effect was forcing them to admit committing a crime.

Even before winning the landmark ruling, Grosso claimed he had retired from the numbers business—the same claim he made at his trial on state gambling charges five years earlier, and many a time thereafter.

In reality, though, his empire kept getting bigger.

"I could name so many crooked policemen and politicians that came up the ladder and rose to fame. We had a way and we both made money," he once told reporters. "I spoke their language and they spoke my language."

But how much of that was true? How much fantasy? No one will ever know.

Yet, as Pittsburghers learned in the 1970s, among the people who did speak Grosso's language was a law enforcement official who had gone to great lengths to portray a pristine public image to cover his sordid private life—the district attorney himself.

\* \* \*

The way Allegheny County DA Robert W. Duggan behaved in the late 1960s and the first few years of the following decade, more than one constituent was led to believe that Pittsburgh was under siege by barbarian hordes from the sexual revolution, and that only Duggan could vanquish the enemy.

Ostensibly, Duggan was a tireless crusader. Hardly a week went by when newspapers and television stations weren't held captive by his well-orchestrated efforts to keep sexual filth from tempting the souls and darkening the minds of Pittsburghers. Much like Maloney and his marauders went after bookies in the fifties, Duggan and his detective squad hounded purveyors of pornography and other sexual pleasures.

He fancied himself the Eliot Ness in the war on commercialized sex. He shut down massage parlors, personally; he led his detectives in charges on newsstands displaying sexually explicit magazines; he obtained injunctions against theaters showing scenes of naked women.

Of course, all this public railing served a convenient political purpose. Duggan was most ambitious, a self-made patrician who had been eyeing the governor's mansion, and he intended for the office of district attorney to get him there.

But while trumpeting the raids on filth, Duggan was leading a queer private life—literally. In certain Pittsburgh and Florida bars that catered to closet gays, and on special occasions in Westmoreland County where he actually resided, Duggan dressed in women's clothes and hosted sexual orgies for elite men friends. He was known with disdain by the open gay community as Dixie Duggan of the Piss-Elegant Set.

Meantime, Duggan was building a personal fortune from disguised "campaign contributions" of cash in paper sacks collected by his detectives. Duggan bought an estate in the Westmoreland County countryside around Ligonier, and a seaside hideaway in Florida. He shook down movie houses and hookers to supplement protection payments from Grosso, who knew about the DA's secret passions.

By the late 1960s, Grosso's operation had evolved into a criminal network of telephones as well as runners. Phones not only gave Grosso's operation speed, but also helped it grow by geometrical proportions. His organization became so large that smaller gambling ventures needed him for layoffs.

Grosso was raking in so much cash that no amount of wagering could break him. His operation had extended well beyond Pittsburgh's city limits and even the boundary lines of Allegheny County. He was proud of his contribution to the local Pittsburgh economy when its legitimate lifeline, the steel industry, was being ravaged by strikes and the influx of foreign steel. "I gave people jobs," he proudly boasted, raising himself above the level of U.S. Steel and J & L managers.

His wealth enabled him to deal with competitors in ruthless fashion. Not unlike the corporate takeover artists of the 1980s, Grosso forced smaller operators into doing business with him even when they wanted to handle their own bets. He did it nonviolently, but persuasively.

Sometimes his people would place so many bets with rivals that when numbers hit, the rival was forced to collapse. And when that didn't work, Grosso relied on a cop on the take to harass the competitor into submission.

Duggan's squad of detectives became part of Grosso's enforcement apparatus in the suburbs. Just as Maloney and his marauders took Grosso's money to turn a blind eye toward Grosso while driving the competition out of the city, so did Duggan and his detectives do the same thing in steel towns along the Mon Valley, in the decaying boroughs and townships along the Allegheny River, and in the established bedroom communities stretching west between the Golden Triangle and Greater Pittsburgh International Airport.

While Grosso was extending the reach of his numbers operation with the help of the DA, and while Duggan was guarding Pittsburgh from the sexual revolution, Congress was putting the finishing touches on a new law that ultimately would undo them both— Duggan permanently, and Grosso, as usual, temporarily.

That law gave federal agents the power to eavesdrop on telephone conversations. Legal wiretapping enabled the FBI to document Grosso's operation as no previous investigation ever could because the evidence was admissible in court. In the past, raids on a bookie's lair yielded enough evidence—

spreadsheets, betting slips, and cash—to arrest the people present. Sometimes, with any luck, the feds could convince one or two of the suspects to cooperate in the prosecution of their superiors, the mid-level managers.

But Sam Grosso, the brains of the family business, had set up the burgeoning empire in a way that often would frustrate attempts to prosecute higher-ups. The Grossos' organization was composed of cells of workers whose duties were so segregated that they had little contact with—or even knowledge of—most everyone else in the group, above or below. The increased reliance on telephones made it even easier to isolate individual cells of workers from the rest of the organization, particularly those in highest positions. Women who took bets on the phone might only know a few runners who called in with the day's wagers and the person to whom the tallies were reported. The ladies had no idea who was at the top. Like the feds, the ladies could only suspect.

Wiretapping enabled the FBI to calculate the Grosso organization's gross income. Together with other evidence, the tapes enabled then-U.S. Attorney Richard L. Thornburgh to spearhead a grand jury investigation that in 1971 brought down Grosso and forty of his highest-ranking aides.

Grosso was convicted and sentenced to ten years in prison. This time, a successful appeal was unlikely; for the first time in his long criminal career, Grosso faced serious time behind bars.

But just as he did with Maloney, Grosso was ready to play his ace in the hole. Only this time, he had an entire deck of cards to offer the eager federal agents.

The first to go were detectives on the DA's racket squad. They pleaded guilty through an assortment of deals that required them to testify against their boss, Racket Squad Leader Samuel G. Ferraro.

Although Ferraro, by this time, had left Duggan's employ for a cushy politically obtained job as public safety director of Hampton Township, he still was the DA's chief bagman. When the feds squeezed him, Ferraro squealed on *his* boss.

One morning in March of 1973, the glib and zealous federal prosecutor, Thornburgh, scheduled a news conference. Although the nature of the announcement was not made public, reporters already knew that Thornburgh was prepared to unveil the indictment of Duggan on multiple charges of extortion and tax evasion. Thornburgh had tipped them off the day before, so they could alert their editors and reserve a lot of space in the papers, and a lot of airtime on TV.

But hours before the news conference, reporters got an even bigger story: near a split-rail fence that ran around his expansive estate in Ligonier, Duggan was found dead; a $7,000 Parker shotgun lay near his corpse.

Duggan's house had been ransacked before investigators arrived at the scene. Some said that the position of the shotgun raised doubts that Duggan's lethal wound in the chest had been self-inflicted.

It remains a mystery to this day, like the death of Don Hughes almost thirteen years later.

After performing the autopsy at the request of state police, Allegheny County Coroner Cyril H. Wecht—a bitter and vociferous political opponent of Duggan—ruled the district attorney's wound was self-inflicted, but did not render any conclusion as to whether it was intentional or accidental. The ruling permitted Duggan to receive a Catholic funeral.

Thornburgh went on to get convictions against others on Grosso's pad—notably Frank Bruno, a bagman who once was a deputy sheriff and then a city justice of the peace.

Thornburgh's stunning success in toppling so many local law enforcement and judicial officers positioned him for his loftier political aspirations.

It proved rewarding for Grosso as well. In 1975, having served twenty-eight months of his ten-year prison term largely in hotels while giving statements to the FBI, Grosso was released. Thornburgh took no stand on Grosso's request for early parole.

And the beat went on.

\* \* \*

Just across from the sprawling South Hills Shopping Center in Bethel Park one evening in late November of 1978, the popular supper club called The Living Room, owned by Angela Grosso, had been doing a typically light trade for a Sunday. Unbeknownst to the suburbanites who dined in dim light while the soft sounds of a piano played in the background, eight men were sitting around a table in a back room behind an unobtrusive door and sharing a repast as the owner's husband held court.

They had been summoned by Tony Grosso, their boss, for an unusual and unexpected demand. Each bookie, he told them, was to pay a monthly tribute from his share of the total wagers they handled, or face arrest by the state police. As a grand jury later heard from one of the participants, one bookie who scoffed found troopers kicking down the door to his headquarters exactly one month later.

The demand for a percentage of their "salaries" was an unprecedented "tax" on men whose overhead previously had consisted of protection payments for cops, bail and fines for runners, and payouts on winning bets. This new expense was an unpleasant surprise. The tribute, Grosso claimed, would go toward the costs that Richard L. Thornburgh had incurred that year to become governor of Pennsylvania.

No one knows where the money really went—and no one bothered to find out.

Seven years after the meeting, Thornburgh's fund-raiser for the 1978 campaign, Pittsburgh attorney Evans Rose, Jr., emphatically denied—in lawyer lingo—that Grosso ever had contributed a penny. Although Thornburgh himself did not publicly address the disclosure of Grosso's demand, Rose said, "To my knowledge, Tony Grosso made no donations to the campaign." Indeed, campaign records showed that not a dime of the thousands of dollars that bankrolled Thornburgh's election that year had come from Grosso.

Yet, back in 1978, the bookies were in no position to challenge Grosso's blatant ultimatum. By then, Grosso had established the illusion that he not only was a baron of the gambling underworld, but also a kingmaker of public officials.

He didn't even need a publicist to create that image; newspaper reporters were only too eager to oblige.

By the time that backroom gathering had

occurred, in 1978, over linguini and red wine in The Living Room, Grosso's role as a contributor of financial support to, and public support for, aspiring pols had long been chronicled.

The first publicity surfaced in the heated fall campaign between Thornburgh and Pete Flaherty, whose reputation as Pittsburgh's cost-cutting mayor won him the Democratic nomination for governor.

The news flash involved a ridiculously trivial incident that was as over-publicized as it was ultimately mysterious. As the Pittsburgh Steelers hosted the Cleveland Browns in early September, 1978, a small airplane trailing anti-Flaherty streamers buzzed above Three Rivers Stadium.

The streamers cried, "A Nitwit Ruined Pittsburgh," and "Mafia's Wango Capizzi Hosts Pete Fund-Raiser at VIP Club." The latter banner referred to mobster Anthony "Wango" Capizzi, an underworld backer of several discos, including a Shadyside nightspot that Flaherty kept from opening a few years before the gubernatorial campaign. Capizzi also was a silent partner in the VIP Club in Bridgeville—which had been reserved for a special fund-raising party for Flaherty a few weeks earlier. The event was called off two days before it was to take place after Flaherty's campaign honchos received an anonymous call informing them that persons of questionable repute would be attending.

The airplane stunt was widely reported and became the celebrated highlight of what political writers called a series of "dirty tricks" in the Thornburgh-Flaherty contest. The others included pamphlets carrying the "nitwit" allegation against the Pittsburgh mayor and a small picket line manned by blacks who had gathered in front of the Stanley Theater during a special Flaherty political fete featuring black entertainer Ben Vereen. The pickets accused Vereen of "selling his people down the river."

Flaherty railed against Thornburgh for trying to sabotage his campaign, but the would-be Republican governor denied the charge.

Then, anonymous calls to newspapers led reporters to speculate openly that the dirty tricks were financed by Grosso himself.

Grosso denied the charges, but only barely. Instead, he took the opportunity of the reporters' requests for comment to publicly ridicule Flaherty and endorse Thornburgh. "They're all liars," Grosso said of politicians generally. "But he's the champ. Pete better watch out they don't put him in jail. He ruined Pittsburgh and the bridges; he'll ruin the state." Simultaneously, he praised Thornburgh, whom, he said, "I got to know when he put me in jail."

"I hold no vendetta," he told any reporter who listened—and they all did with gusto. "I think he'll be a wonderful governor."

"I promised him my support five years ago," Grosso said. "In my years of association with political and government employees, Thornburgh strikes me as one of the most honest, trustworthy, and sincere public servants. You cannot buy him."

What's this? reporters wondered in print. The 'retired' racketeer supporting the campaign of the man who leveled his multi-million-dollar empire?

An embarrassed Thornburgh condemned Grosso's support and joined Flaherty in calling on Allegheny County District Attorney Robert E. Colville and then-U.S. Attorney Robert Cindrich to investigate the dirty tricks. They said they did, but without success.

Meanwhile, Thornburgh charged that Grosso had plotted a sly strategy of reverse-psychology to generate voter support for Flaherty.

Other revelations followed, including Grosso's cash donations to Frank Rizzo, then the controversial law-and-order mayor of Philadelphia, and to U.S. Senator Edward Brooke of Massachusetts, a state where Grosso had allies.

He endorsed other politicians, too. He

called DA Colville "damned honest." Reporters with a sense of history pointed out to
readers that there had been testimony during
Grosso's 1972 federal trial implicating
Colville's father, Robert Butzler, in payoffs
during Duggan's early tenure as district attorney. Butzler, who preceded shake-down
artist Ferraro as racket squad chief, never
was indicted and went on to become chief of
Ross Township police. Butzler was a friend of
state Republican Committee powerbroker
Elsie Hillman, a Thornburgh mentor. Her
close friend, attorney Wendell Freeland, represented many Grosso underlings when they
were arrested.

Grosso also praised other Democratic officials, calling Coroner Wecht "a helluva good
man." He said Allegheny County Commissioner Tom Foerster and Mayor Richard
Caliguiri "know what makes news—like going out and digging a ditch for yourself for a
good picture." Whether he was being particularly astute, or just making a good guess,
was hard to tell.

Grosso, the sage, wallowed in the limelight that went with his silly political musings. He had courted media attention for
years.

In October of 1977, his mug appeared on
the cover of *Pittsburgh Magazine*, which did
a takeout that consisted largely of his deceiv-

ing self-portrait as a man who had walked on
the wrong side of the law for many years but
who had seen the error of his ways.

As he became the focus of almost as much
attention during the gubernatorial campaign
as the candidates were receiving, Grosso further embellished his public image by casting
himself as a benefactor of Franciscan priests
and a behind-the-scenes player in politics.

In one extraordinarily audacious interview
in the *Post-Gazette*, Grosso predicted that
Steeler football star Andy Russell would run
for sheriff of Allegheny County, and teammate Rocky Bleier would become a county
commissioner.

Neither ran for anything but an end zone.

But no one called Grosso's bluff. He was
always accessible, and reporters knew he
would return calls within minutes if he
wasn't around when they first phoned.

Grosso also bragged that *Pittsburgh Magazine* had achieved record sales when it put
him on the cover, that he was writing his autobiography, that he was trying to get "60
Minutes" to air a segment about him, and
that he was soon to fly to Hollywood to negotiate a movie about himself that would cast Al
Pacino or Frank Sinatra in the lead role.

None of this was even remotely true.

More than the media's attention, Grosso
lusted for public recognition as a kingmaker.

Seven years after the *Post-Gazette* article, Grosso, in another interview, said he "made Thornburgh governor" in 1978—and bitterly remarked that Thornburgh snubbed him later. In a lengthy but disjointed story, he said he had enabled Republican Thornburgh to get elected by visiting Democratic party chairmen in populous regions of Pennsylvania and securing their pledge to keep voter turnout low in November among registered Democrats. Grosso contended that the chairmen owed him favors in return for his past financial support.

The political operatives he named in the interview were in no position to challenge Grosso: every one of them was dead. Election results on a county-by-county basis did not support Grosso's claims.

But fact mattered not a whit to Grosso.

Reporters kept knocking on his door and ringing his telephone. Accustomed to writing stories or airing broadcasts about mobsters who never spoke so much as a "no comment," the newsies were ecstatic over the opportunity to interview a real-life, big-time hood willing to speak so freely. And the publicity-hungry numbers boss was only too happy to oblige them.

When the Pennsylvania Lottery was rocked by scandal in 1981, as the number "666" was fixed to hit, Grosso suggested that he was the person who should run a clean lottery. He sat beside television news anchor Bill Burns and provided insight on how the lottery had been rigged, according to what Grosso said he had "heard" from his former numbers associates. He was "retired," Grosso quickly interjected.

While he was honing his image as a racketeer reborn, Grosso also managed to keep his more practiced skills sharp. In 1979, he stalemated the feds again, using his cunning combination of mock innocence and seeming cooperation to blunt an attack by the IRS.

Based on the financial records seized by the FBI in the early 1970s that detailed the volume of Grosso's business, the IRS estimated that he owed more than $30 million in back income taxes.

The agency tried to seize the Mt. Lebanon house, The Living Room, two shopping centers, an apartment building, and several car washes as part of its effort to force Grosso to pay his debt. But the liens were appealed; Grosso argued that he had no assets in his own name and that everything the IRS had been eyeing was solely in the name of wife Angela.

In a hearing before U.S. Tax Court in 1979, the couple argued that the numbers business was Tony's exclusive affair; Angela said she knew nothing about it.

In fact, she said, she knew "nothing or very little" about her hubby's business from the time she began dating him thirty-nine years earlier as a kid in the neighborhood where they both grew up. "My parents evidently thought he was from a good family," she testified in explaining why she was permitted to date the young hood.

"I have to try to remember this," Mrs. Grosso testified patiently. "When I first married my husband, he had a brother that he was involved with, an older brother (Sam, the brains of the operation). Now what their business was, I guess it was gambling. I don't know."

She was asked to review each of her tax statements, and she quietly, dutifully, explained how her annual income swelled from a few thousand dollars to more than $120,000 as a result of the success of her businesses— which, she said, she obtained either through cash gifts or wise investments at an early age. As for whether she asked her husband what he did for a livelihood even after some of his celebrated arrests, Mrs. Grosso replied, "If I did, he wouldn't tell me anyhow, so I never did. Because I wasn't involved, I didn't have any reason to ask him. I didn't care what he did. I had my own little thing and he had his, and you just don't ask people like that any questions. The only time I would know was if he got in trouble, and then I would do just what a wife would do, stick by him."

Grosso himself amplified on the arrangement during his testimony.

"Well, you see, under the Italian custom, we have a way of not telling our wives anything," he testified. "We don't want to hurt them. We don't want to cheapen them. We believe as long as they don't know, and we pay the bills, that's all. My job is as keeper of my home, or part keeper, to pay my wife's bills and keep her happy."

Grosso went on to claim that the miles of adding machine tape and wiretap transcripts from the 1972 FBI gambling case painted a misleading picture of extravagant wealth.

"The numbers business is run on paper only. It's not money. And over a period of the day, like say I was to take in $75,000. I didn't take in the cash. I took in the paper."

Grosso further explained in nearly dizzying fashion that one would have to discount the bettors who welshed, payments on the numbers that hit, people who stole from him, and other undocumented overhead.

"You have your wages, you would have your police department, contributions toward politics, people that steal your money, bonds, lawyers, fines, people that don't pay you. My God, if I had this kind of money that you're supposed to say I have," he told the court, "why you wouldn't have to work. I'd think the whole country wouldn't have to work."

Whenever he discussed his business, Grosso always wove into the testimony enough clumsy expressions to make him appear befuddled by all the legal uproar.

The ruse complimented the silver-tongued eloquence and sharp-eyed skill of the finest lawyers that he—or anyone—could buy.

In 1980, Tax Court Judge C. Moxley Featherston declared, "It is reasonable that Anthony, as he so testified, refused to discuss the details of his illegal activities with Angela. She did not know the location of his business, the number of his employees, the volume of the business, or any other details."

Calling Mrs. Grosso "an experienced businesswoman," the judge said her mate understandably "did not want to expose her or himself to the danger of informing her of the details" of his business operation, and that the tax law's "innocent spouse doctrine" absolved a wife from liability on a joint tax return if she lacked full and specific knowledge of her husband's sources of income.

The same year, the Grossos and a friend, a priest from Boston, were stopped by U.S. Customs agents on the way back from Italy. Inspectors found nearly twenty thousand dollars in cash in the Grossos' luggage and charged them with failing to declare such a large amount. Grosso got a year probation; Angela was turned loose. She hadn't known a thing about the money.

The Tax Court decision and the subsequent 666 scandal that shook the Pennsylvania Lottery in 1981 appeared to signify that Grosso would spend his remaining days as a loveable and eminently quotable retired rascal who had outgrown his life of crime.

He seemed likely to succeed in perpetuating the image of a career scoundrel who finally had been rehabilitated and now just wanted to provide the government with the benefit of his expertise in running lotteries while illuminating voter and pol alike with his observations about the elective process.

He had arrived, pulling off the biggest con job of his career.

And it almost worked.

But Grosso couldn't stay away from the one thing he learned as a newsboy hawking rubbers and digits. He couldn't stay away from the easy buck.

\* \* \*

In a dilapidated mobile home-turned-office that sat discreetly behind the state police barracks in Robinson Township near Greater Pittsburgh International Airport, a squad of undercover agents continuously fought a losing war against vice in a vast area of southwestern Pennsylvania.

Their job was frustrating, given the climate of public acceptance of gambling and the wink-of-an-eye sentences their targets received in court. It got more frustrating in 1982.

By then, the state police were the only large law enforcement agency in the Pittsburgh area that was concerned about illegal gambling. The Pittsburgh Police Department's vice operation had been reduced to a handful of men; the feds had long ago abandoned any serious investigative efforts involving gambling; Allegheny County's detective branch had relegated its anti-gambling endeavors to arresting an occasional numbers runner when one was tripped over.

While the troopers had legal authority to eavesdrop on telephone conversations, that power was limited. But they had another weapon in their electronic warfare against gambling operations, which by now relied almost exclusively on telephones to conduct any substantial business.

That device, a pen register, counted the number of incoming and outgoing calls on any given telephone, as well as the phone numbers being dialed on the line.

Once investigators obtained a court order to install a pen register on a suspect's line, they could almost sit back and let the device do all the work. It didn't matter whether they were on duty or off; the machine ran by itself, churning out miles of ticker tape that would reveal the phone patterns of a bookie.

By monitoring the volume of calls, what numbers are dialed, and the time, the pen register often provides police with probable cause for warrants to search a gambling network's headquarters.

In May of 1982, Trooper Gerald E. Fielder, a burly, bearded, gruff-talking investigator who looked more like a logger, was checking out the results from his latest investigation. A certified wiretap expert for the special vice force, Fielder had been eyeing three suspected bookies in Carnegie Borough and Scott Township in Pittsburgh's South Hills. For the first ten days of that month, the pen registers were spitting out the results expected from a bookie's phone.

Several hundred calls a day were being placed at the times of day that corresponded to the normal closing of a typical numbers operation—an hour before the final bell of the New York Stock Exchange at four o'clock, and an hour before the State Lottery number was picked at seven that evening. Bets were being turned in to banks by bookies.

Fielder was not prepared for the surprise that came on May 11, when the volume of calls on the three telephones plunged by nearly eighty percent. Baffled, Fielder called his snitch.

The stoolie, the same informant who had turned Fielder on to the case, had some disturbing news. "They know you have pen registers . . . in Carnegie," the informant revealed, proceeding to tell the trooper the precise locations.

There was more. Two suspects had been relieved of duty at the bank until the heat cooled off, and the third had diverted most of his business to associates. Someone with accurate inside information about the investigation was leaking it "only to the inner circle of writers," the snitch said.

Fielder didn't know what to make of the tip. He talked cautiously to his partners, but they, too, couldn't understand how. Only a handful of people knew about the pen registers and they all were sworn to secrecy, and to uphold the law. Their occupations ranged from cops who did the leg work to prosecutors who handled the paperwork to the judges who authorized the bugs.

Surely, Fielder and his partners thought, there was a simpler and more innocent reason.

Some bookies switched phones routinely, to avoid giving investigators enough time to develop the information they needed for a warrant.

In October of 1982, however, Fielder's worst fears were confirmed. He and other partners were wiretapping phone lines tied to a large multi-county sports betting operation involving several South Hills and Beaver County gamblers. As they eavesdropped on one conversation, an Erie racketeer named Francis "Bolo" Dovishaw laughed about how a numbers operation near Pittsburgh had access to the confidential police intelligence.

The troopers were astounded when Dovishaw mentioned his information was coming from "T. G."

Those initials stood for only one person, as far as Fielder and his partners were concerned—someone skilled at luring their weaker brethren and tempting them into doing his bidding.

The signs were unmistakable. It looked like Tony Grosso hadn't retired after all. He was still king, still the inveterate liar and corrupter.

But who the hell was his confederate? Who was the Judas with the badge? Who could they trust?

They couldn't ask Dovishaw. On January 1, 1983, his body was found with a bullet in the head. Later, three men were charged with killing him in a matter unrelated to Grosso. Dovishaw's criminal activities went beyond bookmaking.

The worried troopers went to District Attorney Colville, whose office had helped them secure the court orders for the electronic surveillance. With the help of only two of Colville's trusted prosecutors, Fielder's men set a series of traps that were designed to point them in the mole's direction.

But the traps only eliminated some of the possible suspects—principally the three employees from Bell of Pennsylvania who had given technical aid in the electronic surveillance. Colville himself was satisfied his own people were clean.

The troopers were not so sure. As far as they were concerned, the traps were not designed to flush out a prosecutor, or someone from the city vice squad who could have been privy to the original wiretap affidavits.

Further exacerbating their worries was the discovery that the city vice squad's gambling probes also had been contaminated by leaks. The city sleuths distrusted the DA even more than their state police counterparts— and Colville once was superintendent of the city police force.

As one source explained, the paranoia among the gambling investigators ran as high as it did among gamblers. "An incident like this makes everyone look over their shoulders. It's like the KGB and CIA."

Though both police agencies weren't sure of each other's motives and loyalties, they agreed that a grand jury might unravel the mystery.

The panel in 1983 focused on two major bookies. One was a pleasant-looking, chain-smoking housewife from Shaler Township named Mary Pavlick. The other was Norman Fabec, a near-midget father of five and building contractor who lived a few blocks away in neighboring Hampton Township in a home that had a built-in swimming pool and two huge stone lions flanking the entry to the driveway.

Both had been raided in early 1982. The raids turned up evidence showing each handled hundreds of thousands of dollars in bets each week, signifying they were bankers in a broad-scaled operation.

More significantly, Pavlick had phone numbers registered to Grosso himself. And Fabec not only had done business with some of the oldest veterans from past Grosso operations, but also had a list of places under investigation by the state police.

Pavlick and Fabec were summoned to the grand jury and given immunity—a legal maneuver designed to force them to cooperate. But the housewife and the contractor refused to say anything. They were sent to jail for contempt of court to reconsider their silence, but the order was stayed by an appeal.

Fabec later told reporters he had no idea why everyone thought he was involved with

Grosso; Pavlick said she was an innocent bystander.

"We're both pawns caught in a big battle,"
she said. "They wanted me to tell who hired
me. I could have given them that name because the guy died a year ago. They asked
me if I knew Tony Grosso. That's one thing I
could answer. I wouldn't even know what
Tony Grosso looked like if I hadn't seen him
on TV."

Meanwhile, the snail's pace of the hunt for
the mole had put the investigators on edge.
The troopers still weren't so sure that
Colville's office was clean. And they had
stopped cooperating with the city vice squad
on all gambling cases.

By December of 1983, the county grand
jury expired without finding the source of
the leaks. Fabec and Pavlick hadn't spent
more than a few hours in jail. Now that the
grand jury had expired, there was no legal
means to put them in jail because the contempt citations, still under appeal, had been
rendered moot by the panel's expiration.

Colville said he planned to start up another panel, but Fielder and his fellow troopers had other plans. They decided it was
time to go to someone else for help.

They took their suspicions to state Attor
ney General LeRoy Zimmerman. Although
sympathetic, Zimmerman did not share the

troopers' suspicions about Colville's office. Nor was he impressed by the state police's own efforts to ensure that the mole was not a trooper.

It was no big surprise that the troopers' high command in Harrisburg initially dismissed that possibility.

The agency was headed by former FBI agent James Dunn, with whom Governor Thornburgh had worked while a federal prosecutor ten years earlier. Dunn was a consummate pencil-pushing bureaucrat whose accomplishments as a federal lawman were limited to solving bank robberies after local police had apprehended the stickup men. After his successful career as a G-man, Dunn became Thornburgh's yes-man.

With his mania for secrecy, Thornburgh needed someone like Dunn—someone who knew how to keep a lid on controversy and treat the governor as royalty.

When Thornburgh began using state cops to drive his children back and forth to their exclusive schools in New England, Dunn furnished the chauffeurs. When black troopers complained they were victims of discrimination, Dunn transferred them to remote barracks. When Thornburgh wanted to surround himself with bodyguards, Dunn assigned them—then ordered that any information about them, their number, or their duties, be withheld from the taxpayers. The order only convinced Thornburgh watchers that the troopers were private servants, not public ones.

Dunn took little interest in the possibility that the source of the leaks to gamblers might be a trooper. When no one could deny any longer that Fielder and his partners were being sold out, Dunn made a brief trip to Washington County for a chat with the barracks commander.

Just before he died in 1984, Dunn declared himself satisfied no leak existed among his men.

Even before Zimmerman began his own investigation of the leaks, the troopers who worked with Colville's office on the case turned up a disturbing suggestion that ultimately became impossible for the state attorney general to ignore. In late 1983, the elite vice squad from Robinson Township had been investigating a well-known gambling den in Canonsburg where as much as $100,000 was being wagered nightly in dice games that attracted high rollers from several states.

The vice squad was working with plainclothesmen from Troop B, stationed in Washington County. In the Byzantine structure of the state police, vice investigations were conducted by two separate outfits on two separate levels. The organized crime force, the one stationed in Robinson, operated on a regional level and focused primarily on large gambling operations. Small-fry hookers and street bookies belonged to plainclothes officers assigned to every barracks. But often both units cooperated in large investigations.

The elite squads routinely exchanged intelligence with various local barracks, since there always was a chance that one prostitute or one bookie might lead up the ladder.

Such was the case in the investigation of the Canonsburg gambling den. But each time the organized crime troopers planned a raid, they arrived only to find the place empty. At Colville's suggestion, Fielder and his partner changed their routine: they executed a raid without telling undercover investigators from Troop B.

The raid went like a charm.

Troop B investigators also had been cooperating with the Robinson Township crew in an investigation of Grosso's nephew, Joseph Grosso, Jr. Once they obtained a court order for a pen register on the younger Grosso's phones, they ran into a dead-end that had become all too familiar by 1983: the phone calls dropped to a trickle.

Because of his powers as state attorney general, Zimmerman could order an investigation that crossed county lines. Puzzled by

the experiences involving Troop B, his prosecutors and a statewide grand jury began fo-
cusing on the Washington barracks. By mid-
1984, the investigation turned up astonishing
information.

Informants who were given immunity testified that Tony Grosso was rumored to have
many troopers in his pocket to keep him
abreast of any investigative activity. By that
time, Colville had started a new grand jury,
but opted against any more mole hunts. Instead, his prosecutors turned up the heat on
Grosso himself, while Zimmerman's office
began a closer look at the Washington barracks.

By late 1984, Colville and Zimmerman
were convinced that the leaks came out of
the Washington barracks. They narrowed
their list of suspects to a group of four or five
plainclothes troopers who had been seen eating dinner on several occasions at The Living
Room.

That group of troopers, informants
claimed, had accepted other small gratuities
besides free meals. But by early 1985, as the
separate probes by the DA and attorney general were closing in, investigators also were
convinced of one other thing: among the
small group who supped at Grosso's table,
one trooper did a lot more than stuff his face.

\* \* \*

When he graduated from the State Police Academy in Hershey in 1960, Donald P. Hughes was a trooper with a mission. He wasn't content to pull light duty assignments on the Turnpike or fill a chair behind a desk. As soon as he could, he put in for duty on criminal investigations, eager to serve the state's top law enforcement agency like a macho crimebuster.

By 1976, he had worked his way up to head of the Troop B vice unit in the Washington barracks. He not only liaisoned with the elite vice squad in Robinson Township, but also had access to investigative intelligence data from undercover troopers in Allegheny and four adjacent counties.

For more than ten years, he had dealt with scores of sleazebags, turning them into informants in his pursuit of bigger game. One day in June of 1980, Hughes flipped the biggest fish of his life. He called Grosso at The Living Room and suggested they meet at the bar in the South Hills Sheraton Hotel, located a stone's throw from The Living Room.

Grosso readily agreed. For four months, he claimed, he was Hughes' personal snitch, fingering bookies who could be busted after

only a few weeks of not-so-difficult detective
work.

"He loved to brag and he loved to talk
about putting this man in jail, that man.
He was good in what he did," Grosso said of
the tall, lean, corporal for whom he had
become an informant. In reality, Hughes
was nothing more than a tool for punishing
Grosso's sticky-fingered staff, or an upstart
competitor.

It didn't take long for Hughes to fall into
the trap that had sucked in Maloney, Duggan, Ferraro, and countless others.

As Grosso remembered the familiar script:

"He started talking about me paying politicians; me paying this, paying that. I said,
'Look, I did pay a lot of people, but that's
all.' "

Then, with a slightly discernable smile, he
added, "But I think he knew I was a good
man with police."

One afternoon while they met in a dimly
lit corner of the Sheraton bar, Grosso took
out ten $100 bills and laid them on the table
in front of Hughes. The corporal protested,
"No, no, no," all the time reaching his hand
out to cover the bills.

The bills disappeared from the table and
the two men sealed their pact. As Grosso understood the terms: "He was supposed to
feed me. If I wanted somebody knocked off,

he'd knock them off. If I wanted him, I'd call and he'd meet me."

"It gave me a little power," Grosso explained, adding that after the troopers would bust a wayward bookie, "I'd go to him." The visit would make the busted bookie a loyal part of the Grosso operation. It was an offer that couldn't be refused.

At first, Hughes' "salary" was $1,000 a month. In no time, it went up to $2,000. A year or so had passed when Hughes announced to Grosso that he wanted to buy a bar. "Let's stop kidding ourselves," he said. "I want this."

Hughes' price was $100,000, paid in two installments four months apart. In addition to that sum, he still collected his $2,000-a-month salary—as well as free paid vacations to Florida for him and his wife.

The conspirators met each month, but in a room at the Sheraton instead of the bar. Grosso insisted their meetings just didn't involve dollars and numbers. "We developed what I thought was a friendship," Grosso recalled, saying he sometimes would give Hughes candy to take to his wife.

But Hughes, a father of three, had other meaningful friendships as well, especially with a woman who was his wife's best friend. Besides lining his own pockets, Hughes got Grosso to pay for a fence for the girlfriend's yard, and rooms at the Sheraton for afternoon trysts.

Grosso thrived on blackmail-caliber tidbits involving sexual exploits.

Sometimes Grosso would invite Hughes home. "He would pull into the garage and we'd sit and talk for one or two hours," Grosso remembered with an air of fondness.

Hughes also was Grosso's wedge for controlling Fabec, the Hampton bookie who in 1983 was prepared to go to jail rather than testify before the grand jury that was probing the leaks. Always suspicious of even his closest aides, Grosso believed that Fabec was skimming from the operation.

Fabec, who became Grosso's right-hand man after Sam Grosso died in 1979, had tried to take over the whole organization by becoming another trooper's informant. But the double-cross was neutralized by Hughes, who passed along to Grosso the information that Fabec gave to the state police. The tip enabled Grosso to circumvent trouble with the uncorrupted lawmen.

"Everything Fabec did I found out from Don Hughes," said Grosso. "Fabec didn't even know about Don Hughes. Nobody knew about him but me. It was a secret."

But not entirely.

During the May, 1982, wiretap that first tipped Fielder off to the possibility of a leak,

Hughes had warned Grosso that Pat Petraglia, one of Grosso's oldest workers, was under state police surveillance.

Grosso said he would warn Petraglia, unswayed by Hughes' pleas that doing so could tip off investigators to his betrayal. "I couldn't see hurting a lady who was seventy years old. He didn't want me to do that," Grosso, the softie, explained.

Hughes was right.

After Grosso warned her, Petraglia warned her three closest aides—the three people whom Fielder had under surveillance. One of the aides was Petraglia's son, Bobby Levy, rumored to be Grosso's illegitimate son from Grosso's brief dalliance with Petraglia during their long association in the rackets.

Grosso later called his tip to Petraglia his worst mistake.

As the hunt for the mole intensified, Hughes kept urging Grosso to keep his mouth shut. Perhaps realizing that he was no less vulnerable than Maloney and Duggan and all the others had been, Hughes also tried to browbeat Grosso. "He told me he'd call me a liar and could beat me in any court in the country. Then he started telling me he got a family with kids and that his wife would leave him."

But cops and their families mattered little to Grosso.

He figured they knew the risks. What did matter to him was his numbers operation. And by late 1983, with the mole hunt only just beginning, Hughes began looking like a bad investment for Grosso.

With the heat turned up—through raids to which Hughes was not privy—Grosso began wondering what he was getting for his protection payments. "I told him if he can, stop sending these raids out. He said he didn't think he could. It looked to me like he just didn't care, like he thought I wasn't going to bother with him and he wasn't going to bother with me."

Then, one frigid day in January of 1985, the two met for the final time. During a meeting at a small motel near the Washington barracks, Hughes asked Grosso to strip. He wanted to be sure that Grosso wasn't wired.

Hughes had reason to be concerned. Colville's grand jury already had charged Grosso and Fabec with running a numbers operation that investigators estimated was doing $25 million a year in Allegheny County alone.

Grosso angrily recalled the meeting, repeatedly mentioning how cold he was as he shivered in the unheated motel room, stripped down to his scivvies to allay Hughes' suspicions. Grosso's recollection of his physical discomfort was not the only reason for his anger as he talked about his last meeting with Hughes. He said his feelings were hurt. But he really was humiliated by the trooper's audacity. Here he was, Tony Grosso, numbers baron and kingmaker, stripped down to boxer shorts and T-shirt at the behest of a cop he owned.

"I gave him all this money and he didn't trust me," Grosso recalled in an interview. His face hardened with a scowl as he continued: "I had no intention of giving him up, but I was so bitter after he had me stripping and everything."

So Grosso paid Hughes his last $2,000 and went home to make the familiar call: he phoned his lawyer and told him to cut a deal.

Colville and Zimmerman were coordinating their investigations. Grosso was able to negotiate yet another sweet surrender. In return for pleading guilty to the new charges that Colville's grand jury had filed, Grosso would receive ten years probation if he appeared before Zimmerman's grand jury and coughed up Hughes.

Hughes was reassigned to clerical duties in February of 1985, and the following August he was arrested by Zimmerman's office. By the beginning of spring, he was history.

Although he never gave his own account of his relationship with Grosso, Hughes acted out a familiar story, even in death.

After his body was discovered by his wife, there were suggestions by her that Hughes might have had help dying. Much ado was made over four bruises on his head, although the Washington County coroner's office said they could have resulted from the way the corpse had been handled, or from Hughes' falling once he had been overcome by carbon monoxide. The bruises ultimately were determined inconsequential, and Don Hughes became a statistic alongside the late DA Duggan, whose death occurred under mysterious circumstances in the spring of 1973. The common denominator—Anthony M. Grosso, survivor.

Shortly after his own arrest, Grosso lamented, "I never should have bothered with Hughes.

"He didn't care, as long as he got money."

Of course, Grosso cared only as much. And that ultimately led to his own undoing.

Shortly after Hughes' demise, Fielder and his partners worked with Colville's grand jury and arrested Grosso and Fabec again. Then, a federal grand jury indicted them for tax fraud.

In October of 1986, Grosso pleaded guilty to the federal and state charges. Suffering from cancer of the colon, he told U.S. District Judge Donald Ziegler that he never got much of the money the government said he did. "My wife supports me," he said.

Within a few days he received a six-year sentence as Ziegler called him a bookmaker who "was much more" than a bookie. "He has corrupted. He introduced an element of bribery into bookmaking and he did it on a grand scale," the judge intoned.

Common Pleas Judge Alan S. Penkower then all but insured Grosso would pass away behind bars, imposing a ten-year prison term to begin upon parole from the federal penitentiary.

Grosso looked pale and drawn.

Ultimately brought down by the greed he had exploited in others for nearly half a century, Grosso seemed to have lost his glib repartee.

He looked up at the judge and said, "I don't feel so good."

Some people felt just dandy.

▲

# Fading Out

By Abby Mendelson

Well, sir, the bluegrass craze gave out, and so did his back. The Dog Run Boys busted up, and, finally, Rick Malis just got tired of the road.

He's older now, 39, and there's silver in his hair. But his round, mustachioed face still has a puckish pull to it, and his soft tenor is still as high and sweet as mountain air. And he's still writing those sad, sad songs.

Born and raised in blue-collar Lawrence, Massachusetts, Malis was hit young and hard by Tom Rush, James Taylor, and Paul Simon. So, he picked up the guitar and taught himself a passel of songs. He came to Pittsburgh for college, from which he took a degree in English, and his guitar, and set off to sing.

For a spell he lived the vagabond poet's life, farming, hammering and sawing, even teaching. And singing, his mournful tenor naturally lending itself to plaintive country and bluegrass songs—songs with the bare-boned emotion, the pervading sense of loss and yearning in the souls of people who've tasted the knuckle sandwiches of life.

Malis traveled, playing coffee houses, on his own and later with bands like Windy Ridge, Stony Lonesome, Rodeo Smoke, the Bluefield Boys. They all came and went until the Dog Run Boys. Named for the road that ran by Malis' Washington County farm, the Dog Run Boys lasted from 1979 until 1985, and made Malis—the on-stage leader, writer and arranger, booker and business manager—one of the area's top folk performers.

Comprised of four musicians, including folkscene fixture Bob Artis on mandolin, the group played in virtually every bluegrass bar and concert hall in the tri-state, from impromptu jams in Stu Cohen's Walnut Street Music Emporium to gigs at Graffiti, and scores of stops in between. Soon the Dog Run Boys had a sizable following and were playing festivals as far as Minnesota. "We were doing very well," Malis recalls. "Maybe *too* well. We'd hear standards like 'Fox on the Run' four hundred times," he says and shakes his head. "It was maddening." Devotees remember that Malis took his revenge by penning a wickedly funny send-up of intermarriage called "Lox on a Bun."

Over the years they evolved from a band that lived on winging it—"instantaneous arrangements," Malis calls them—to an "original group which stressed new as well as traditional material. We were eclectic—

and fun—and so attracted a real hip, urban crowd."

Maybe the group could have gone bright lights if it had moved to Nashville, say, but like many, Malis preferred to stay. "You can be a good songwriter from anywhere," he says, "and I really like it and am comfortable here. I love the feel of Pittsburgh. That's very important. Besides, the Dog Run Boys were really embraced. It was almost like we had a responsibility to the town."

Yet, slowly, inexorably, the scene shifted away from bluegrass. Tastes changed, venues closed, band members sought other things to do. For his part, Malis needed back surgery, which made lengthy driving and standing impossible. "It was getting tougher and tougher," Malis remembers. "It was like trying to fit a circle into a square."

Since the Boys disbanded, Malis' bad back has kept him off stage—and he's not sorry. "I got my taste," he says. "I played almost every Saturday night for more than twelve years. And I really enjoyed it."

Now he's content to be a part-time songwriter. "I never wanted to be a full-time musician," he says. "I never liked the travel, and I never wanted to perform seven days a week. That takes enormous energy and emotional commitment. I got into music for the right reasons—I love it and it was fun. If I did it full-time that would stop."

Currently a Gateway Studios' special projects vice president, Malis writes mostly in his modest Forest Hills home, which, perched on a tree-lined hilltop, seems as woodsy as some of his tunes. Malis works them out on a '47 Martin, scratching out lyrics on a yellow pad. These days he has about five dozen songs he's proud enough to show, about forty percent of which he's copyrighted. Some have been published in Nashville, some Malis has put on a cassette demo called *Not a Day Slips By.*

Although he slides into pop and contemporary now and again, his major work is still folk and bluegrass, adding modern settings and themes to traditional ideas. "Life isn't that simple or clear," he says. "I always see the undercurrents—and try to use ambiguity."

Some of his more poignant, imaginative songs: "Jenny Brown," full of minor chords and dark memories of a mismatched love affair and loveless marriage, and "Living on the Bottom Line," an up-from-under look at trying to make it.

A new one called "Blue Highway" centers on the haunting memory of a former lover:

> Looking at all the drifters and losers,
> I'd still wake and find you on my mind.

Blue highway,
Take me far from you.

Malis breaks into a piece of a song called "For Better or Worse." "Right or wrong," he sings, high and lonesome, like the best of bluegrass, "she's long gone—for better or worse."

It's got the right bite, the right feel of sadness, the right chords. Malis shakes his head again. "I've been working on it for two months and I just have bits and pieces. I don't have it all. It's hard. To write good stuff I have to find ways to rekindle the fire."

# Irv and the Ivories

## By Adrian McCoy

A cab driver picked up William Steinberg, the conductor of the Pittsburgh Symphony, in front of Webster Hall Hotel one night in the late sixties. On the ride downtown, he asked Steinberg for a ticket to the next performance. Steinberg complied. The cabby was Irving Broner, a piano player whose improvised barroom rhapsodies might have given the maestro pause.

Irv used to play in cocktail lounges, but his isn't just the lounge pianist's slippery stylings or sloppy backdrop for sing-alongs. It's a crucible that fuses all the things that drew him to music: the classics, Spanish music, Tin Pan Alley. He drifts seamlessly from classical to Cole Porter. No matter how sadly out of tune or whipped the piano, he can make it sing.

What stands out are his "rhapsodies." Irv can turn just about anything into a rhapsody.

Although he doesn't play jazz, his approach is similar: he takes a standard like "Night and Day" or "Someone to Watch Over Me" as a starting point, leaves the melody far behind, and rockets off into the ether. Where he took it was sometimes so amazing that even the audience members who were two sheets to the wind had to notice.

Irv deserved nicer instruments, a bigger, better stage, and a polite, paying audience. His concert hall was wherever there was a piano and some people.

He often played at a little bar called Delaney's on Craig Street in Oakland. A night at Delaney's was an experience. It was the classic tear-in-your beer kind of place, where the jukebox oozed weepy country tunes and pop songs. People spilled their guts and told their troubles and sometimes even burst into song. It was like a stage musical version of *The Iceman Cometh*.

George Delaney, who owned the place and tended bar there for more than twenty years, was the spirit of congeniality. He treated everyone like a guest. From the outside, it looked like a hole in the wall. Inside, it was clean and cheerful. It looked like time had stopped in 1951. It even had a crystal chandelier. George would take it down occasionally and carefully clean all the pieces.

"Delaney ran a class place," Irv says.

Delaney's even had its own alleged ghost—a woman dressed as a flapper who stood at the bar and called out for "Harry." A man named Harry supposedly was killed there when the place was a speakeasy in the 1920s.

"Diamond" Lil Seddon played piano there on weekends. Lil, who was in her eighties, cut quite a figure, attired in an awe-inspiring beehive hairdo and a couple pounds of rhinestones. She pounded out ragtime versions of standards like "Bye, Bye, Blackbird" and "When Irish Eyes Are Smiling." She hit the occasional wrong note, but it was always the same one every time she played it, so it sounded right after awhile. She always nursed a glass of beer—on the rocks. When Irv was there, he'd sit in during Lil's breaks.

The crowd was an oil-and-water mix of neighborhood old-timers, punk rockers filling up on inexpensive drinks before heading out to the clubs, and the disenfranchised, who found a place where they sort of fit in. What they all had in common was a love of cheap beer. After about eleven o'clock, this motley crowd would gather around Lil at the piano and sing "Danny Boy," even if they didn't know the words.

George is gone now, and so is Lil. Delaney's was sold in 1985, and has gone through several reincarnations. These days, it's a sushi bar.

Irv says Beethoven is his favorite composer, with Brahms running a close second.

He saw a statue of Beethoven in Volkwein's one day. He bought it and used to drag it around to bars where he played.

"I like Cole Porter. I love his lyrics. He wrote poetry. And George Gershwin and Jerome Kern, or course. These guys were the greats."

It gets his goat that people like Madonna make millions, while Bartok and Beethoven died in poverty.

Irv was born in the Hill District in 1923. His father was a broom peddler who came here from Palestine in 1905. Irv was one of six children.

His musical story started when he was about thirteen. He took piano lessons for six months from a woman who would come to the house every Saturday afternoon. The lessons cost a quarter.

One fall afternoon he was playing football in the street. The teacher came over to coax him inside for a lesson. She ended up intercepting a pass and getting tackled. She never came back.

But it wasn't the end for the fledgling musician. Irv learned to play bass and was in the All City Orchestra during high school. He took a course in harmony at Allderdice. Building on those foundations, he learned to create his own piano arrangements, many of which he figured out using sheet music with only the melody and guitar chords.

He watched other piano players. "I picked up on my own from different people. Buddies taught me this and that."

He's written about thirty compositions— popular songs, novelty tunes, and semi-classical music. He went to New York in 1955 to make the rounds of the music publishing houses, working as a proofreader by day. He met a lot of talkers and heard a lot of promises, but nothing happened.

He came home in '59 to take care of his father, who was dying of cancer. Irv worked at a variety of jobs, including cab driver, furniture mover, and cook. At nights, he'd play the piano at several places, most of which are only memories now: the Hop 'n Scotch on Grant Street, the Silhouette Lounge in Dormont, Cicero's in Oakland. In the late '70s, he played on Saturdays for the residents of an East End nursing home.

Playing piano in saloons meant fighting against loud jukeboxes. He walked out on his job at Hop 'n Scotch over it. He didn't have carfare, so he stormed home on foot—up Bigelow Boulevard, hauling a pile of sheet music, the statue of Ludwig, and a gooseneck lamp.

These days Irv doesn't play much. He doesn't own a piano. When he can, he plays a beaten old spinet at the American Legion Hall in Squirrel Hill. When people ask him where he's playing next, he says, "I turned my fingers in."

That's not quite true. For old times' sake, he played some of the old Delaney's favorites on a quiet Sunday afternoon recently at the Legion Hall—dreamlike interpretations of "Malaguena" and "Orchids in the Moonlight" that should be preserved on tape somewhere.

There's no place to turn in a gift like that.

# Walk-In Sculptures

By Abby Mendelson

He's 50 now, an age when most architects look for ways to expand their staff—and get off the board. Yet Arthur Lubetz recently cut the number of his employees in half, to six, to get back to what he set out to do. "I wanted more hands-on control of things," he says. "I wanted to be more selective about my work. Because what matters is not how many people you have and how much you do, it's the quality of what you do with the people you have."

Tall, with a silver ponytail and a loud, expressive voice, Lubetz has maintained his own firm—and singular architectural vision—since 1968. Known for his dramatic use of form, color, and space, Lubetz' architecture is influenced by the city's topography, its hills and rivers, the looming shapes of its industrial past.

Lubetz' work is muscled and manly. Planes dissect each other, calling out in bright, primary colors. Red walls slash abruptly through buildings. Elemental materials—glass block, steel beams, exposed ductwork—break up and redefine space. Walls come halfway up, or down, offering mute sermons on the laws of gravity. In perhaps his single boldest and most humorous statement, a two-story yellow pencil pierces the older, false facade of the Top Notch art supply building on South Craig Street.

A Pittsburgh native, the son of a used-car and auto parts dealer, Lubetz lives a hundred yards from the Shadyside house where he was raised. An artist since his childhood, Lubetz chose architecture after a visit to Carnegie Tech. After graduation, he stayed in Pittsburgh, wanting his own practice, hoping that hometown connections might bring commissions. More than two decades later, with but two projects coming from people he knew before college, Lubetz realized how illusory that idea was.

"I stayed for the wrong reasons," he says as he shakes his head. "In fact, staying here might not have been the smartest move I ever made. I regret saying that because I love this city. But I'm convinced I would have had more opportunities somewhere else. Because there's a very narrow view about what's accepted, what's good."

While he had been much praised by critics for his design, Lubetz laments that "there isn't a market for the kind of work we do." Certainly, he has done many notable—and highly visible—projects, from Squirrel Hill townhouses to the Monroeville Islamic Center. Yet most are small, relatively low-budget affairs. Big buildings—and big commissions—have escaped him.

That may be because his work, here and elsewhere, is immediately recognizable. "That's very important," he says. "We practice architecture as a public art. We want to make people aware of architecture, and by extension, the world around them."

His own office on North Craig Street is a good example. Lubetz stepped off an old three-story building, cutting it into layers going uphill, making a clever mix of multiple entrances and interior open space. Although much of the building is rented to others, Lubetz' quarters on two front floors contain offices, more or less, a conference room, and an airy two-story work room.

A personal watershed was Morehead Tower, a highrise for the blind. Lubetz' challenge was to use different floor coverings, light and air sources, and building materials so that blind residents could experience the building non-visually. The experience was so powerful, Lubetz says, "it changed my outlook on architecture."

"People imagine my buildings are expensive," he adds. "They're not. The work is more important than the money."

One measure of his cost-effectiveness is the number of institutions, speculative buildings, and contractors' homes he has designed. For the Mistick house on Lincoln Avenue in Allegheny West, Lubetz had the occupants write what they wanted. The themes that kept recurring were family, sunlight, and space.

In keeping with their comments and the demands of the historic district, Lubetz recreated an original street frontage. Then he had a computer track the sun—an updating of what ancient cultures did—and designed an interior sun-yellow curved wall that follows the sun's path. A smaller, darker, wall tracks the moon.

Then, with typical Lubetzian panache, he split the house in half, into male and female sides. On the male side, the structure is uncovered—black steel beams protrude above the roof suggesting the city's industrial past and Mistick's profession as a contractor. On the female side, the structure is covered. The two children's rooms are appendages on opposite sides of the house. Children come and go, he says.

Depending on client input, and approvals, a finished design can take as few as ten days—or as many as eighteen months. The Mistick house, for example, took months, generating a two-inch stack of sketches. The winnowing process, Lubetz says, "made the house a lot better."

"I believe in the importance of architecture," he adds, "and in what I do. And what I do is not easy, in terms of work and financial reward. But I like it. It feels good. I get a lot of artistic and intellectual fulfillment out of it, out of making a small contribution."

As such, he has no unfulfilled plans, no sheaf of unmade projects. "My work is very site-specific and client-specific," he says. "It relies on clients pushing at me and me pulling at them. I enjoy the reality of what I do."

▲

# When to Quit

By Roy McHugh

It was one of those amateur boxing tournaments the Allegheny Mountain Association promoted every year in the 1960s. Al Quaill had entered a team from his gym on the South Side and he was working in a middleweight's corner. Halfway through the second round, the kid stopped defending himself. He turned his back on his opponent and signalled that he'd had enough. Quaill looked embarrassed and sick.

He could not understand a fighter who just simply gave up.

In 1938, at Hickey Park in Millvale, Oscar Rankins hit Quaill so hard that the punch fractured his sternum. When the bell rang to start the next round, the fifth, Quaill was unable to raise his hands. His trainer had to do it for him and repeat that routine at the start of every subsequent round. Quaill fought on, and the decision was a draw.

Quaill had the conviction that no one could beat him. During his first year in the ring, he saw Frankie Battaglia, one of the top-rated middleweights of the day, lose to

Babe Risko. "I can lick that Battaglia," Quaill
told his manager, Chappy Goldstein. Quaill
kept repeating this until Goldstein believed
it too. In his thirteenth professional fight,
Quaill's opponent was Frankie Battaglia.

Later Quaill said that his scouting of Battaglia had been faulty. A hoodlum named
Frankie Carbo controlled the middleweight
division at the time, and when Carbo took an
interest in any given fight the performance of
the fighters was apt to be unpredictable.
Quaill always had the idea that Carbo took an
interest in the Battaglia-Risko fight.

At any rate, the Battaglia who confronted
Quaill in Motor Square Garden one night
was not the same Battaglia who lost to Risko.
Quaill remembered nothing distinctly after
the first time Battaglia knocked him down.
"Everything went black," he said.

At one point, momentarily, the lights came
back on. He looked across the ring and noticed Battaglia kneeling. "Why, that louse,"
Quaill said to himself. "He's been beating me
to a pulp and now he's resting." Quaill did
not realize that he had just put Battaglia
down.

In the sixth round, Battaglia knocked
Quaill through the ropes, and he climbed
back in with the help of a spectator. The
spectator was Quaill's brother Tom. "What a
favor he did me," Quaill used to say. "He

pushed me back in there, and Battaglia knocked me out cold."

Solidly put together, Quaill had the build of a football lineman, which, at South Hills High School, he was. He took up boxing when his coach recommended a strenuous summertime activity. No form of athletic competition is as elemental as boxing, and Quaill liked it better than football.

Quaill had fifty fights all told. He lost only eight, with two draws, but quit the ring young, at 25. He was losing the sight of one eye, and though boxing commission doctors were tolerant then, and Quaill carried bravery to a remarkable extreme, his plans for the future did not include total blindness.

As a city policeman for thirty years, he cheerfully risked life and limb. In 1946, off-duty, he was driving past the site of a Teamster election when it suddenly turned into a shoot-em-up. Quaill stopped his car, ran into the crowd, unarmed, and grabbed a .32-caliber revolver from a man who had pumped five slugs into five of his fellow union members.

To Quaill it was evident that the youth of America should know how to box. Boxing develops self-confidence. Self-confidence enables one to act in a crisis. Quaill believed that. In various gyms around town, he always had amateurs learning. He would not allow most of them inside a ring, but he was glad to teach anyone the fundamentals.

Whether actual experience disillusioned him, Quaill never said. He died in his fifties still teaching. Perhaps he thought, and perhaps rightly so, that he had toughened the fiber of his students. But whatever it is that makes an Al Quaill can probably not be acquired.

▲

# The Critic's Choice

## By Abby Mendelson

The proposed Shadyside historic district is an odd patchwork sprawling between Aiken and Neville Avenues, and architectural historian Walter Kidney is here to make a surgical diagnosis.

Inheritor of Jamie Van Trump's role as Pittsburgh's collective memory and prose stylist, Kidney, 58, is tall and ungainly, with fingers that seem to stray all over the landscape. A kind and scholarly man, he is given to vests, bemused chuckles, and great curved pipes that give off only slightly less smoke and ash than the J&L Hazelwood stack.

Kidney works for the Pittsburgh History and Landmarks Foundation, and has written numerous books, including *Allegheny, The Three Rivers,* and *Landmark Architecture: Pittsburgh and Allegheny County,* a catalogue of virtually every major building in the area, with an insightful—and often quite droll—comment on each.

The son of a teacher, Kidney discovered architecture one summer day when he was seven. Spotting an ionic porch capital on a neighbor's house, he was fascinated and eager to learn more. "I had always been interested in objects," Kidney recalls, "things that were designed and constructed, such as ships, locomotives, and so forth. There is a sense in my family that this should be a very orderly world. Machinery, properly designed, and visually appealing buildings have that sense of order."

Although he liked Pittsburgh and its buildings, he migrated a bit, to Haverford College, Random House (where he worked on the *Random House Dictionary*), and points east and west. He came back for good twelve years ago.

In his Mount Washington apartment Kidney slouches at a large table, pipe nearly on his chest, banging away with his right index finger at an old manual typewriter. ("I like something I can beat on," he says.) An exacting self-editor, Kidney works over his typescripts, amending, often adding copious longhand notes.

Yet he has left his notebook home this morning as he surveys the ravages of time and careless owners in Shadyside West. Walking erect down Wallingford Street, he points out turn-of-the-century houses that have been stripped of porches, had spacious bay windows bricked up or replaced with smaller fill-ins, acquired ill-considered facades, and so on.

This sun porch was added some seventy years ago, Kidney says. That staunch brick house has had a garage dug into its belly. And that one, there, is a nightmare of decaying ornament—filigree and fish-scale shingle and who-knows-what-else? "The Victorians saw the picturesque in isolation," he explains. "The moderns see buildings as a whole, with all the features subordinated."

Yet it is the moderns, or more appropriately the contemporaries, who are wreaking such havoc, and who must be stopped before the tattered neighborhood is ruined entirely, he argues. There are in-fill, suburban-style houses "with no relationship to the roof pitches or masses of the houses around them," Kidney says. Where the newer houses have tried to copy the older, stronger styles, they have failed. Cheap pastiches, they have neither the proportion nor the style of their ancestors. "They lack self-respect," Kidney sniffs.

One disaster, pink brick with ersatz gaslights and ill-proportioned windows, especially annoys him. "It's a bastard house," Kidney says. "Not only are its blood lines impure, but it is not cherished by anybody—especially the one who fashioned it."

Hence the unfortunate device of historic designation, which, if made into law, will regulate future changes in the neighborhood.

"It's a vote of no-confidence in modern building," he says, "architecture, planning, development. Historical preservation is necessary now. Otherwise you're going to get chaos. You want to preserve the spirit and the architecture, so you still feel you're in Pittsburgh."

What he hopes will return to Shadyside West are houses with character and dignity. Not cliches—circular windows are a particular anathema—but strength, clarity. He gestures at a house with strong lines and ornamental shingles around the windows. "It's so simple," he says, "so well proportioned. It could be a model for new houses in the area. So could the quietly modern." In other words, the real thing—of any age.

"Buildings have impressed themselves on Pittsburgh," he adds. "For example, the Cathedral of Learning. It was large and meant to show the public, the sons of working men, that there was a better life through education, that blue-collar life wasn't inevitable.

"The Cathedral is a rhetorical gesture," Kidney continues. "What I like about Pittsburgh is the dramatic quality of the terrain, how it stimulates your imagination. It's a three-dimensional city. Even though most of our architecture is rather drab and commonplace, if you put it in a setting where the streets are constantly rising and falling, on a ridge or in a valley, or looking out great distances, the whole thing becomes very romantic—it becomes enlivened by that spatial quality. Sometimes you wouldn't really want to go and look at what's out there on that hillside. Yet at the same time it's so marvelous to see it from a distance. And from that hillside you see another marvelous scene somewhere else. It all means that there's a slightly illusory quality about Pittsburgh, that somehow it's better to look at the neighborhood from far away than from within."

# Making the Most of It

## By Vince Leonard

He sashays across the railroad tracks onto River Road. His flop hat is tight on his head against the cold. And there is the long overcoat, and the splotched denim apron sticking out a couple inches below. The apron's for work and, well, for the cold, too. He carries a brown shopping bag by one handle. It is filled with shoes. To friends in passing cars, he raises the bag in salute, maybe five, six times.

Before entering the shop, he looks down on some wild ducks gargling glop where the Chartiers Creek flows into the Ohio River, wishing he could reach them with crusts of bread. He can't. And shrugs.

He pulls open the screen door of his shop, retrieves the morning paper which is folded and standing upright in the corner, kicks loose a wedge of wood, sticks a worn key in the lock, opens the door, and enters the World of Edward Kenneth Lewis, the Duke of Shine.

"They don't know me by my whole name," he says in a little drawl, a thin smile tightening into gentle concern on a round, brown face with misty eyes. "They know me by Kenny."

So it is Kenny's World in McKees Rocks, Pennsylvania, spitting distance from the Golden Triangle of downtown Pittsburgh.

Kenny is 74, stooped, and a shiner of shoes for the last thirty years.

"Because I like it," he says. "Sometimes I sit here all day and don't make one shine. If you want to know the truth, some weeks I don't make five dollars. I stick around here 'cause I'm old."

Kenny moved from Columbus to Pittsburgh forty years ago "to heat rivets" for Pressed Steel Car Company. "That lasted three years," he says, "so afterwards I had to start shining shoes."

Inside his shop, a converted railroad car mounted sturdily on concrete blocks, there is a stand that can accommodate four pairs of feet, a stove, a television set, and a couple of chairs, all dominant fixtures. The rest is clutter.

Customers sit on a pew-like bench, worn to a polish by the seats of their pants. There are tattered girlie books in the corners, and rags underneath.

Six hours a day, seven days a week, this is where Kenny stays. Working or waiting for work or loafing, it doesn't matter what you call it.

When he works, he toils. Often a bead of

sweat forms on his bald head and drops onto the shoe. Kenny buffs it away; it improves the shine.

Kenny worries about such things as a genuine spit shine. And he worries about his image. "If you call me anything but Kenny, you'll ruin my personality."

And he makes delicious malapropisms: "I don't want to detonate (downgrade) the town because it's where I live and work—but thirty years ago the town was blooming."

In about the time it takes to polish a pair of shoes the right way, Kenny tells the rest of his life's story.

"Shining shoes is back-breaking work but you've got to get used to it. And you get better at it, just by asking questions of other people. You know you can go 'round and see things. You see something on display at a shine stand and you want to know what it is. You go get it and try it out yourself and you see how it works out. Then you have something extra for yourself, too.

"Some places in the old days you used to get a shine for a nickel. My regular price is fifty cents now, but I usually take what they give me. My biggest tip might be a dollar. I never get celebrities, just common people. You get those big men Downtown.

"The secret to a good shine is lots of polish and hard rubbing. Some others just dab it on, take it off, and tell you 'that's it.' You're supposed to take your time, just like you would putting your necktie on.

"Same as you want to look nice yourself, you want the other fellow to look nice.

"In here most of the talk is about girls or the lottery. The time of day, the weather, sports, that's all. Sometimes a man sits beside another man and strikes up a conversation about politics. But mostly they talk about girls. That's the best, don't you think?

"Nothing's here now. Nothing's like it was thirty years ago. I could make love thirty years ago.

"Nobody likes to shine shoes anymore. If they don't make four hundred or five hundred a week, they don't want to work. It isn't what you make, it's how you spend it. You take what's coming to you.

"That's better than going out and holding up people."

▲

# A
# Nonconformist

By Abby Mendelson

Ezra Pound, held prisoner by the American military, is trying to set up a pup tent. As played by Pittsburgh actor Bingo O'Malley, Pound is weary, irascible, sarcastic. Using a black soldier as a foil, Pound calls him Kingfish, Amos, Rochester, Booker T. When the soldier holds up a dictionary, Pound asks him if he's trying to learn a second language.

Director Jed Harris sits, smoking, and two prompters lounge nearby. A group of overturned tables substitutes for a set in the open, empty basement of the Foster Memorial. It's early in rehearsals. Both actors miss lines and have to be reminded.

Harris interrupts. Youthful and energetic, he works on nuance, sight lines, blocking. O'Malley nods, pliable, incorporating Harris' direction as he goes.

As the confrontation builds between Pound and the soldier, and Pound talks about art, language, and Florence, he becomes increasingly animated, first prone, then sitting, finally standing. Pound fills with energy as he speaks about the power of culture. Harris stops him, encouraging O'Malley to reach a little farther, to stretch a bit.

A lanky man with a wintery face—weathered skin, bright blue eyes and gray hair and beard—O'Malley, 56, is bundled in a dark, army-style coat, work shirt, and jeans (*everybody* at rehearsal wears jeans). He's trod the boards for two decades now—untrained in acting, a chance encounter with a Key West theater company, and a part in *The Rainmaker*, turned him to the stage.

Born and raised in Oakland, O'Malley's worked as a juvenile probation officer, served as a Diocesan priest, and, for the past seventeen years, a Pittsburgh public school psychiatric social worker. It's a job which, like his theater work, he finds engrossing, demanding, and deeply satisfying.

Having a day job, however, makes life extremely difficult during the three or four times a year O'Malley's in plays. A creature of exhaustion, O'Malley fights through his weeks on four hours sleep a night. Crawling into bed at 1:00 in the morning, facing a 5:30 alarm, he often asks himself, "What am I doing it for?"

Perhaps it is the distinguished series of roles he's had at the City Theater, Lab Theater, Pitt, and others, in such plays as *American Buffalo, Glengarry Glen Ross, Nuts,*

*John Kane* (for which he shaved off his trademark beard), and *Carnegie*. Oddly, he's never worked for the Public Theater, in part because PPT rehearses during the day. "We haven't been able to get together," he explains, and shrugs.

He acts, he says, "because I like to express myself, or have an emotional release, or explore myself—all the hackneyed things." O'Malley shakes his head. "Most of the time I don't know. I do love the process—having a part in making something, then following it through to completion."

Although most of his work is in the theater, O'Malley's done commercials, and worked in a dozen or so visiting films, *Creepshow, Dominick and Eugene*, and others. "If I feel like it," he says, "I do one. But I don't have to do something I don't want to."

While other Pittsburgh actors have left, and done well, O'Malley prefers to stay. "Go where—and do what?" he asks. "I haven't wanted to go. My roots are here. I'm a Pittsburgher by nationality. People look for measures of success outside themselves—who they are, where they live, who their friends are. For them, fame is a matter of numbers—ten people or ten million, two dollars or a million dollars. But I like Pittsburgh," he counters, "the topography, the work ethic, the simple, old-time values."

He has taken those values, reached inside himself, and become the consummate Pittsburgh actor, a strong stage presence and resonant voice, a man with range and humanity without pretense, without ego.

O'Malley has excelled in projecting that part of himself on stage, notably in his portrayals of painter John Kane, and › Andrew Carnegie. As the steel magnate, O'Malley "explored the other side of a business tycoon," he says, "finding humanity in the ogre."

Doing *Carnegie* was particularly rewarding, he says, because the play brought a whole new group of people to the theater, including steel workers and people who remembered the bloody Homestead Steel strike. They sought out O'Malley afterward talking about the play, sharing their memories. "To get that kind of feedback," he says, "and feel the play come alive in so many ways, wouldn't happen in bigger places. That's not just a matter of recognition. There's a connection with the past, going on to the future—a continuum—you don't find anywhere else."

*Incommunicado*, an unsettling story of Ezra Pound, has given O'Malley one of his most cerebral roles. A poet, Fascist, and virulent anti-semite, Pound made defamatory speeches on Italian radio during World War

II. Arrested by the Allies and held in a psychiatric hospital, Pound, lover of Italy and editor of T. S. Eliot, suffered a nervous breakdown and a protracted recovery. "We deal so much in absolutes," O'Malley says. "Here, my role is to try to understand Pound, to see if he was a good person."

Back on stage, the scene is clicking. O'Malley has found Pound's rhythm, and, filled with emotion, he rolls, laughs, stands, gestures, jumps. *Now* he has it.

Harris stands. "Bingo," he says, "that feels much better, doesn't it?"

O'Malley's blue eyes sparkle. "Yeah," and he smiles.

▲

# Gross Encounters

## By Paul Maryniak

Measured either by the sheer volume of their crimes or by the antisocial depths to which they sank, the Codfish and his sadistic groupies were perhaps the most vicious, lethal crew brought to justice in America's most liveable city. For admirers of the macabre—the nonfictional and grotesquely funny variety—Snooky, Stretch, Egghead, Monster, and their brutal leader probably were the most laughable homicidal maniacs ever to wear a ball-and-chain.

They botched hits, they blew drug deals, they double-crossed each other, finked on each other, cut each other's throats, shot each other, and even defiled the corpses of their transgressors. They did all this with such consistency, regularity, and vulgarity that one top police official publicly announced that the casualties in their grizzly killing spree amounted to civic improvement. Cameras rolling, he freely told the news media what surely was the unspoken opinion of his colleagues, and then he hastened to add, almost as an afterthought, that the episodes were murders—at least in the technical sense.

It was fortunate they were arrested when they were on that bright warm day in June of 1981. By the time Codfish and the rest of the gang were rounded up in a pre-dawn strike at homes and haunts across the city, they had taken out six men who had been giving different law enforcement agencies embarrassing headaches of varying degrees. Had the murderous lot not been rounded up, the cops risked the possibility that sooner or later the gang would claim a life worth saving. So by June of 1981, Codfish and Company were ready for retirement, for a reward of sorts for their gruesome fix-up community campaign.

Death row awaited the Codfish, and life behind bars most of the others. Prison was far from an alien environment for many of them. It was someplace they went between capers.

Like the dead players in this real-life black comedy, the killers shared a bond beyond their failure to do wrong things the right way. That bond was the gutter, and neither victim nor killer ever rose above the level of certifiable dirtball. Lacking even the fundamental virtue of honor among thieves, the whole crowd gave crime a bad name among professional criminals.

Certainly the case gave informers everywhere a worse reputation—a Keystone

Crooks story too fantastic for Hollywood, with bizarre takes which proved that not every so-called organized crime plot is all that organized, and that inside every big-time hoodlum is a sniveling punk trying to sneak out.

The felonious freakshow featured lurid scenes bereft of any redeeming social value, such as the bloody rub-out of a drug dealer who paid cancer patients pennies for their prescriptions of the pain-relieving medicine Dilaudid. The deranged capitalist sold the narcotic at an exorbitant profit to gang members, who in turn peddled it at a four thousand percent markup to teenagers too sophisticated to stick a needle full of heroin into their veins. The gang's supplier was whacked because of a fatal flaw in his marketing plan: he refused to extend the gang's credit; he wanted cash up front.

And that was as logical as things got.

"Some murders shouldn't be listed under the obituaries. They should be listed under civic improvements," intoned Allegheny County Police Superintendent Robert Kroner, referring to the drug dealer's demise and that of the other victims of the hapless killers. With that statement, the normally reserved and ever-tactful Kroner broke tradition. First a diplomat and then a cop, he was never known to say an unkind word about anybody in public—until June of 1981.

But the case of Pittsburgh's Gang That Couldn't Shoot Straight was full of the unexpected, the unusual.

Kroner's out-of-character blunt comment on the not-so-dearly departed came only hours after the pre-dawn police sweep—one of those raids by federal and local lawmen to which every newspaper reporter, TV personality, and on-the-scene radio play-by-play broadcaster is invited with promises of an exclusive. An accomplished media manipulator, Kroner basked in the publicity that the arrests were accorded by area and out-of-state newspapers.

He conveniently down-played the fact that this gang practically begged to be captured. Their conduct was so brazenly open at times and so utterly mismanaged at others that they were like theatrical characters in a slapstick spoof, The Day the Three Stooges Invaded the Underworld. The gang's trademark—crude foul-ups—was facetiously said to have shamed genuine mobsters into self-imposed exile. The joke was that pros who appreciated finesse in breaking the law were so ashamed that they talked of heisting a truckload of lunch pails and heading out for jobs in the mills. Only by this time, the mills were closing down faster than the victims of the gang were falling. So, the anecdote went, the real gangsters abandoned the dark corners of the nightclubs they secretly owned and, until the media grew tired of the story, the Mafiosi went around in disguise in broad daylight by removing their hats from in front of their faces.

When The Gang That Couldn't Shoot Straight was escorted—paraded, really—in shackles to the morgue for arraignment on murder and other charges, police sharpshooters were perched on rooftops while others hung out of helicopters whirring above Grant Street. This titillated cameramen even though some snickered behind the lenses; insiders were aware the paramilitary poses had been struck for the reporters' and cameramen's benefit because it heightened the dramatic effect. Actually, nobody cared to help these lowlifes escape. And if they tried it themselves, there was no doubt in anyone's mind that they surely would screw it up. But the pizzazz made wonderful copy for print journalists and terrific visuals for the Live Eye and Insta-Cams at six and eleven o'clock.

Everyone bathed in overkill.

The big break in the case had happened routinely, just like most breaks in high-profile cop thrillers: One of the conspirators ratted on the rest.

In this case there were two songbirds who told whodunit, howtheydunit, wheretheydunit, and when—another case solved largely without the good guys ever having to wander too far from the office coffeepot, or stand in the rain.

At first the cops found it hard to believe that the bad guys had managed to scrape up enough intelligence to move huge quantities of marijuana, cocaine, uppers, and downers into Pittsburgh, or that they even knew which way to point a gun.

The cast of characters eventually became so large that programs should have accompanied the media spectacle that police officials had arranged for the gang's initial court proceedings; the audience then could follow who killed whom for what reason. Four of the six killings ended in trial. A snuff in Fayette County was left for mystery fans to figure out for themselves—until, about eight years later, the ever-cautious, win-conscious federal prosecutors decided they could use it to help build a major racketeering case against a big-time mobster in Wheeling. The sixth snuff, the Dilaudid entrepreneur's killing in Florida, prompted Miami area police to file homicide charges against several gang members. But the southern lawmen never began extradition proceedings to get the defendants into the Sunshine State, seemingly content with letting the Commonwealth of Pennsylvania care for the murderers while Florida stocked its death row with local talent.

The defendants for the Pittsburgh extravaganza included Robert "Codfish" Bricker, William "Egghead" Prosdocimo, James Griffen, Miles Gabler, Thomas Skelton, and Charles Rossi. The last two arrested, onetime Pitt football ace Charles Bonasorte and Hazelwood clothing salesman Samuel Rende, were cleared early in the judicial proceedings for insufficient evidence.

Off the record, the dismissal of charges was due to mass confusion.

The thugs' incompetence notwithstanding, their arrests were justifiably a time for rejoicing among many police and federal agents, because some of the adversaries had the temerity to taunt narcotics officers, as if acting out some scene from an old James Cagney movie.

As for the victims, there wasn't much in their backgrounds to send the Chamber of Commerce into mourning.

Perhaps the death least likely to draw applause for flare was Norman McGregor's. He was a thirty-year-old West Mifflin bouncer whose favorite pastime was beating up people; not people exactly, bums like him. His killing involved the most suspects—Bricker, Griffen, Skelton, and Rende. McGregor was drygulched on his front porch.

Raymond Mitchell, Melvin Pike, Phillip Hubbard, Gary DeStefano, and Tommy Sacco shuffled off this mortal coil with few mourners in their wake but a fair amount of flourish. And, as Kroner's public statements indicated, their deaths seemed to mark their first solid contribution to the betterment of society.

No wails of grief echoed through church pews for Mitchell, a North Braddock drifter and petty armed robber who bragged about his crimes too loudly. Griffen, Bricker, and Rossi got credit for his death. It resembled an amateur lobotomy which concluded with a midnight backyard funeral, a la Alfred Hitchcock.

No tears flowed for Pike, a Uniontown extortionist, strong-arm man and a never-charged suspect in several more killings, including the unsolved slaying of a teenage boy whose only mistake was to drive-up on a burglary-in-progress. Bricker and Griffen were identified as Pike's assassins. Pike bought it while the Codfish slurped up a gooey dessert over the body.

No testimonials were issued for Hubbard, the entrepreneur from Alexandria, Virginia, who paid the terminally ill for Dilaudid, which became known as "white man's heroin." Bricker and Prosdocimo were charged in his demise, caused by a gun, a chair leg, and a clothes rack, preceded by the rape of a woman bystander.

No bugles sounded taps for DeStefano, a

Monessen chauffeur for drug dealers who was double-crossed during a drug rip-off that was blamed on Prosdocimo, Bricker, and, at least initially, Bonasorte. DeStefano was drilled in the eyeball and then praised for taking it like a man.

And no flags flew at half mast for Sacco, a Dormont thug and drug dealer shot dead because he got too high and started telling the world he was a police informant—right in front of the informees. Bricker, Gabler, and Prosdocimo were all convicted in this slaying. The blabbermouth Sacco's lips were moving to say something even as he drew his last breath, according to the proud executioner, Codfish.

The cases were solved through the cooperation of two informants, Charles Kellington and Gerald Walls—career felons whose own lives were no less sordid and no more worthy of public commendation.

And, of course, no less hilarious.

They seemed an unlikely pair to be cooperating in anything.

Neither liked the other.

Walls complained that Kellington belched on purpose in front of their women. Kellington thought Walls was a patsy with a big mouth.

Lord knows which nagging flaw was more offensive.

Both had flipped for the government after separate and unrelated arrests. But both went straight for basically the same reason: to protect their respective, but not respectable, hides.

Kellington's strapping six-foot, four-inch, two-hundred-forty-plus-pound frame and methamphetamine-fueled temper had earned him the nickname "Monster." He gave new meaning to the words "fat slob." Each time he lumbered to the witness stand in various court appearances, Kellington looked more uncomfortable in the same ill-fitting white shirt and cheap, thin, tie that the prosecutors made him wear. A bullet-proof vest added another layer to his ugly dimensions. No matter how often he rehearsed for a session on the witness stand, Kellington always looked like he was ready to pick his nose.

Kellington was the most notorious Pittsburgher on the good guys' side of the case. A native of the Uptown district who went to Vietnam shortly after dropping out of Conley Vocational School in 1963, he had been a bartender in dozens of nightspots, and an occasional laborer, until 1969, when he found his true calling—violent crime.

He studied at the feet of a master, Joey DeMarco, a Brookline racketeer whose Court Lounge catered to hoods as well as judges, lawyers, and Grant Street powerbro-

kers, until 1979. His bullet-riddled body was
discovered then in the trunk of a car in the
short-term lot at Greater Pittsburgh International Airport. His slaying closed the per-
fumey Court Lounge and forced the clientele
to find a new watering hole with much less
atmosphere.

As DeMarco's disciple in the early 1970s,
Kellington used ball bats and bulk to collect
gambling debts from deadbeats when he
wasn't hawking stolen goods on the black
market. Kellington thrived on making bones
crunch. He regaled juries with tales of conduct that would be frowned upon even in
Lawrenceville, where he had settled.

He said he once pulverized all fifteen
members of a dance band because "someone
grabbed my old lady's ass."

On a dare, he climbed the fence of the zoo
and shot a deer with a bow and arrow, then
hauled away the carcass as a trophy from his
urban safari.

Arrested twenty times in less than five
years, he confessed to just about every crime
open on the blotter. He was a pimp, thief,
tax cheat, fence, pusher, strong-arm man,
drug addict, welfare fraud artist, conman,
and perjurer. Yet, even though his propensity
for causing pain gained him a reputation of
being a hitman, he claimed he never killed
anyone; rather, he just "didn't discourage

them from thinking that." Another time, he tried to distinguish between drug rip-offs and plain stealing. "I never stuck anybody up, but I'm not an angel," he said with a straight face.

After getting out of prison, where he served a two-year term for selling hot merchandise, Kellington in 1976 fell out with DeMarco because "Joey thought I was a snitch."

As things developed, DeMarco hardly could be faulted for thinking suspiciously. He was a prolific snitch himself. He was on the payroll of four federal and two state agencies simultaneously, without any of them knowing about the others. He sold the same information over and over and over.

It was around then that Kellington developed a voracious appetite for drugs, spending days snorting as much as ten grams—one thousand dollars worth—of cocaine daily. "I wouldn't go to sleep until it was gone," he testified, saying he also took as many as ten Quaaludes a night and washed them down with a fifth of whiskey. He bragged he took amphetamines "like I was eating peanuts." A father of five who admitted never going home for weeks on end, and beating his wife when he did, Kellington eventually suffered the consequences of his appetite. By 1979, he said, "cocaine ate my nose"—not a small accomplishment for the narcotic. He developed a chronic sniffle that punctuated his testimony with nauseating frequency, inhaling bursts of wet air after every comma and period and paragraph.

Kellington put lawmen on the track of The Gang That Couldn't Shoot Straight. Tied to the Hubbard killing, he inadvertently implicated himself in the slayings of McGregor and DeStefano. He was not known as a fast thinker under pressure. The feds warned him they would rather see him go to Florida and face certain electrocution in the Hubbard killing unless he began cooperating. It was legal blackmail, so to speak, but the hulking criminal didn't seem terribly offended. Kellington later testified that it was not so much the death penalty as it was death row in Florida that terrified him. Police said he often talked of how he loathed his year in a Miami cellblock with inmates who only spoke Spanish and were dirty.

What finally pushed Kellington into the willing arms of the police was the same thing that helped contribute to the gang's downfall generally. Kellington said his cohorts turned a deaf ear to his distress call for a "quality lawyer." There seemed little doubt that one reason they ignored him was because they were cheap. As testimony showed in cases involving some of the killings, the gang found people who would murder for as little as a few hundred dollars.

Of course, the killers in some cases botched the job, proving that even the most hardened criminals get only what they pay for.

In the last of his meetings with law enforcement before he finally agreed to tell all, Kellington listened to officers lay out in detail the grim future he faced if he remained tight-lipped. Monster said nothing for a while, then sobbed—although it was never clear whether he was relieved he wouldn't have to face a Cuban cellmate, or whether he just didn't like the idea of walking on the outside with a bull's-eye on his back.

Walls often cried, too. Ironically, he shed a tear for DeStefano, one of the victims of Walls' pals. His grief ultimately made him a credible corroborative witness for Kellington. The unpleasant prospect of prison undoubtedly kindled a small spark of civic responsibility, but there was no question of his value to lawmen in the case.

Walls tattled after he was arrested in a drug raid at a Strip District water plant, caught red-handed with two pounds of cocaine only a few days before he was scheduled to surrender to federal prison authorities to begin a three-year term for counterfeiting.

Unlike Kellington, Walls looked eminently comfortable in the three-piece rose-and-

purple polyester suit that he wore to court.
As perpetually unkempt as Kellington appeared, Walls looked dapper, or at least as
dapper as someone who always lived in gritty
Uniontown could ever hope to become. His
carefully air-blown hair and baby-fat face justified his nickname, "Snooky," and looking at
him conjured up images of someone who
spent the better part of his life hustling cocktail waitresses. Witnesses recalled how Walls
often tried to impress women by telling them
he was a big-time racketeer, sometimes pushing aside his suitcoat to show a gun tucked in
his waistband.

Even on the witness stand, he sounded
like he was trying to pick up bimbos. Only
34 years old at the time the case broke, Walls
never could resist bragging about his underworld activities as "the collection guy" for
Fayette County, controlled by Wheeling
crime boss Paul "No Legs" Hankish. Walls
also referred to himself as a major dealer of
uppers, downers, coke, and weed, for a substantial part of southwestern Pennsylvania.
The secret to his success as a drug dealer was
simple: "Always deal with quality people," he
testified, with the arrogance of an expert scientific witness.

Not that he always followed his own advice. True to his association with a bunch of
reprobates who could screw up jaywalking,

Snooky confessed to no small degree of incompetence as a pusher. "I got ripped off a lot of times," he testified remorsefully. Other times, he spent a small fortune on a wholesale shipment of drugs that was inferior; once, for example, he bought a load of Quaalude tablets that were virtually unsalable because they had been stored in a damp place.

A denizen of the minor league underworld taverns in Uniontown, Walls, in 1967, began a seven-year prison term for hunting down and stabbing a suspected intruder into the office of his mentor, protector, and employer, then state Senator William Duffield. Duffield was also Walls' lawyer.

Long before Duffield was tossed out of the legislature for his conviction on charges of putting ghost employees on his payroll—and later disbarred for stealing money from the estates of some clients—Duffield helped Walls win an early parole. Other than the fact that Duffield and Walls were fellow travelers in the same shady circles, it was never made clear why the Uniontown senator was so publicly helpful. Unless he, too, figured there was a difference between stealing and stealing. It made sense to people like Kellington.

Walls loved high living and flaunting wealth. Once he plunked down $3,400 for a pet cougar that he took along with him when he motored in his Cadillac to Florida to pick up cocaine. He kept a small arsenal of handguns. He fancied himself an irresistible ladies' man—true, but it was among females who on their best day could not be defined as ladies.

Yet, even though he often would casually allude to his romantic adventures, he also portrayed himself on the witness stand as a devoted husband and father.

Jurors would sometimes roll their eyes in disbelief when he explained that he had turned state's evidence because "I wanted to see my two little girls grow up." The defense attorneys who cross-examined him surely would have scored big had they asked Walls, rapid-fire style, to name his daughters without pausing to think.

Neither Walls nor Kellington ever seemed to have grown up until their lives of crime hit a dead-end facing a badge. Their own accounts of life on the wild side made them sound pathetically like boys trying to act tough.

As different as they tried to make themselves seem, Kellington and Walls shared common interests. They both found a mainstay in dope. They frequented the same night spots—especially the Ben Avon Veterans' Club, which was a far piece from Ben Avon.

Before it was torn down to make way for the PPG Building, the Market Square dive was more commonly called Butchie's, in honor of a shrimpy Brookline numbers runner and bartender who, by age 40, had not yet found a reason to learn how to read and write. To impress patrons who clustered around Butchie, no doubt awed by the bartender's success with less than a basic education, Kellington and Walls often bragged about their underworld influence.

They retained that swagger in their many appearances before judges and juries—swaggering, in part, because they had negotiated a twenty-year prison term for a series of misdeeds that normally would have entitled them to life terms. The twenty-year sentence itself was a misnomer; both were out on the streets in a quarter of that time.

If Kellington and, to a lesser extent, Walls were stars for the good guys, Codfish Bricker deserved top billing as the main villain.

In fact, his exploits almost single-handedly merited the gang's title. But then, 40-year-old Bricker, from the North Side, had the best nickname. He pronounced it "Cudfeesh" from "Norside."

Long before he was arrested in June of 1981, Bricker demonstrated a knack for clumsy, hideous crimes.

Nearly two decades earlier, in December of 1963, he tried on his wedding day to find a quick way to pick up a few bucks to finance the honeymoon. Unemployed and on parole from a five-year prison term for robbery, Bricker, just before his nuptials, telephoned a onetime cellmate, McKeesport disc jockey and car dealer Willie Jenkins, and asked for a loan of five hundred dollars. Jenkins agreed to meet in Stanton Heights in an alley, apparently hoping that Bricker intended to resume a pay-as-you-go homosexual liaison they shared in the pen.

Jenkins guessed wrong.

Not only did Bricker have no intentions of infidelity to the bride, he also decided to cancel the loan before the first payment came due. He shot Jenkins twice in the chest, then sped off, dragging the still-breathing and screaming victim beneath the car for about three hundred feet. Bricker never made his honeymoon: Jenkins' screams had been heard by neighbors who called police. Even before he could kiss the bride, Bricker was back in the clink.

Ten years after he pleaded guilty to that rough reunion with Jenkins, in 1964, Bricker's life sentence was commuted by former Governor Milton Shapp. The Pennsylvania Board of Pardons heard Western Penitentiary staffers testify about the "positive strides he has made to better himself." For Shapp and the board, earning a high school diploma, an associate college degree, and a movie projectionist's license while behind bars met the criteria to waive Bricker's remaining debt to society. As it turned out, the Codfish was a little smarter but not better. Considering the scandals that accompanied the Shapp administration, it was small wonder that learning to show movies qualified as a good enough reason to let Bricker's bygones be bygones.

Shapp's legendary abandon in granting clemency was overshadowed by the Pardons Board's visionary assertion that "this man will become a useful member to society."

In light of some of his subsequent activities, maybe the board was right.

At the same time Codfish was rehabilitating at Western Penitentiary, learning about show biz, so were Walls, Rossi, and Mitchell. Bricker picked up almost immediately where he had left off once he tasted freedom.

It was never made certain how he got the nickname. Kellington insisted it was because Bricker was a cold and ruthless killer who attacked on whim—much the same way a codfish acts, or so Kellington, no ichthyologist, explained repeatedly on the witness stand. Public defenders who had the hopeless task of defending Bricker in the killings claimed Kellington's story was a lie and that Bricker was hit in the face by a codfish thrown during a food fight among inmates.

Regardless of the origin of his moniker, the Codfish indeed proved himself a cold-hearted killer within months of his departure from the joint.

As testimony later showed, Bricker returned to his violent ways sometime in September of 1974 when he paid a visit to Raymond Mitchell at a ramshackle house in North Braddock. Bricker was upset that Mitchell had been bragging about various hold-ups that he and the Codfish had committed within the first few months after their parole. Considering such boasts would have changed the minds of even the most liberal member of Shapp's Pardons Board, Bricker originally asked Griffen, a reputed hitman in Wheeling, to find someone who would kill Mitchell. But when he was told it would probably cost five thousand dollars, thrifty Bricker was said to reply, "For that kind of money, I'll do it myself."

Besides being Bricker's onetime cellmate, Rossi was a perfect companion for the trip. He respected Bricker's morals. Rossi had spent most of his adult life in the slammer for killing his landlord. Rossi was eighteen at the time. He, too, was paroled in 1974. Rossi already had spent nearly three decades behind bars. At the time of his arrest in 1981, he—like Bricker—had learned to live an ostensibly honest life; he was working as a counselor at a drug rehabilitation center in Coraopolis. The Codfish was a projectionist at a North Side skin-movie theater.

Griffen was described by police as a stone-cold contract killer who was part of the muscle employed by West Virginia panhandle crime boss "No Legs" Hankish. Among the members of The Gang That Couldn't Shoot Straight, Griffen was the most menacing—and the most mysterious. In several of the killings that were tied to Bricker, Griffen acted as a facilitator—a middleman who knew whom to call if someone wanted someone else dead.

So when this trio of ex-cons knocked on Mitchell's door, there was a strong likelihood the meeting would come to no good for the host. After Mitchell opened the door to the last guests he would ever receive, the trio took him into the basement for a chat. As Rossi later recalled, the four of them began talking, arguing, until Bricker pulled out a .357 Magnum and shot Mitchell in the chest.

Incredibly, Mitchell was still alive, his gaping wound making a chilling sucking sound as he breathed. Bricker walked up and fired again, at his head, the bullet tearing off the victim's scalp. Rossi, whose thick-lensed glasses barely saved him from blindness, pointed at the top of Mitchell's head and shouted, "Look at the rat." Bricker smiled and said, "That's no rat; that's his brain." To illustrate, Bricker reached into the victim's skull through the open top and stuck his fingers through the eye sockets.

He started working the head like a puppet, Kellington later quoted Bricker as boasting.

Bricker buried the body in a garden in Mitchell's backyard, later proclaiming to Kellington he would never bury another corpse because it was too strenuous. Sometimes, Rossi later testified, Bricker would muse about the killing and laugh, saying, "I wonder who's living there now. If only they knew what was in the backyard."

Bricker's inside joke proved his undoing. Although they had not been in Mitchell's basement, Kellington and Walls confessed they had heard Bricker tell the story with vivid recall. With little solid information except that the victim's nickname was "Mitch," county detectives figured out the victim's identity, then exhumed his remains. For the police and prosecutors, the discovery was even better than all the polygraph tests that

Kellington and Walls had passed in their countless debriefings: It proved the two snitches really knew what they were talking about.

Bricker demonstrated more ruthlessness—and his gruesome sense of humor—in the McGregor hit five years after Mitchell's.

He had been given a contract to ice McGregor that summer. The Codfish and his accomplices set out on the job in something less than expert fashion. The first time he tried, Bricker failed miserably. He barged into the Down 'N Under Bar in Homestead in September, 1978, after he had been told his quarry was there, but didn't know what the target looked like. Walls had assumed that after pointing out McGregor to Griffen, that Griffen would do the same for Codfish. Griffen decided he could accurately describe what the target looked like instead of fingering him.

Griffen overestimated his communication skills, or perhaps the Codfish's ability to comprehend the language.

Bricker shot an innocent patron, wounding him in the shoulder with a shotgun. As had been prearranged with Kellington, another middleman in the ten-thousand-dollar contract, Bricker telephoned Monster and whispered a coded message: "The car has been painted."

A few hours later, Kellington called Bricker back and said, "You painted the wrong car."

Over the next three months, Griffen and Walls took Bricker through various bars to point out the target and prevent another botched attempt. Months later, Bricker got his chance to paint the right car. He lurked in a bed of tall weeds across the street from McGregor's West Mifflin house. While McGregor fumbled for his keys in the cold on the front porch, Bricker opened fire with the cheap Italian rifle he had purchased especially for the hit—a weapon he later described proudly to Kellington as "the same kind of gun that killed President Kennedy." As Bricker readied a third shot, McGregor's wife turned on the porch light. The Codfish told his confederates that the light improved his aim immensely. He fired three more times—these with deadly accuracy, and his prey screamed, "Oh my God, I'm hit! Turn off the light!" Kellington said Bricker laughed and laughed about the hit: "He said he died like a punk, that he was praying to God for his life."

Considering the many screwy developments in the case of The Gang That Couldn't Shoot Straight, few observers were surprised when a slightly different version of the McGregor killing emerged after Rossi pleaded guilty in the Mitchell killing and decided to take a seat alongside Walls and Kellington in the federal inmate witness-protection program. Long after Monster and Snooky had testified many times about Bricker's account of how he gunned down McGregor, Rossi took the witness stand in a different case and said the actual killer was someone else, a former Northsider named James "Sonny" Watson.

Rossi claimed that Bricker told him he had hired Watson for $1,800 a few months after Watson had escaped from a West Virginia prison by castrating himself and getting transferred to a mental hospital where he could make his break.

"Bricker said he took credit for it because the person he got the money from thought Bricker did it," Rossi testified. Later adding that, "It was not out of character for Mr. Bricker to take credit for things he didn't do." Rossi said he didn't know Kellington and Walls had been involved in the McGregor killing—or that they had testified Bricker did the job.

None of this conflicting testimony among their star witnesses bothered prosecutors. One nonchalantly said, "There are no inconsistencies in the testimony." They noted that Rossi and the two other snitches essentially provided the same details of McGregor's death—with the minor exception of who caused it, of course—and said that often there are different levels to a conspiracy, that not all conspirators necessarily know all the details of a plot. To the wide-eyed astonishment of Bricker's lawyer in the McGregor case, the judge accepted that argument.

After convicting Bricker, prosecutors then charged Watson as an accessory and convicted the self-made eunuch as well.

It was somewhat surprising that Bricker had been offered the McGregor contract, considering his sloppy execution of Phillip Hubbard in August of that same year in the Newport Hotel just outside Miami.

The Codfish had gone there at the behest of another gang member, William "Egghead" Prosdocimo, a Squirrel Hill drug dealer who looked like a ferret. Prosdocimo was given to kinky sexual acts with both genders. Police found pictures of Prosdocimo leading his naked fiancee by a dog leash as she walked on all fours around a room, and there were stories of conventional homosexual acts without props. He was nicknamed for his egg-shaped skull. Prosdocimo, who dealt primarily marijuana and Dilaudid, was the epitome of cockiness. He often taunted undercover detectives whom he knew—and who knew him— at various places around his Squirrel Hill home. When he was lodged in the county jail with no hope of bond because he was a candidate for the electric chair, Prosdocimo

managed to secure a television set and stereo
for his cell. During his trial in the Sacco killing, Prosdocimo often would sling an arm
over the back of his chair, look over to friends
on hand for moral support, and giggle at various witnesses' testimony. He treated the entire trial as some misbehaving adolescent
would treat a dull high school teacher in
class. The jury taught him a hard lesson,
though, by convicting him of first degree
murder. That wiped the smirk right off Prosdocimo's acne-scarred face, making him bawl
like a baby when the prosecutor began arguing to the same jury to send Eggy to the
chair. The tears worked. He was sentenced
to life imprisonment instead.

At the time of Hubbard's death, however,
Eggy was still the cock of the walk in Squirrel Hill and Hazelwood. The envy of losers in
the neighborhood because he drove an expensive sports car and dressed in designer
clothes, Prosdocimo acted the role of an un-
touchable. He figured the cops weren't
smart enough to touch him—and that his
suppliers had no right to demand payment
on delivery for drugs. He was brash and his
lifestyle fast, so when Hubbard began press-
ing him about an unpaid debt of $6,000 for
Dilaudid, Prosdocimo decided that murder
was cheaper.

Eggy arranged to have Bricker and

Kellington accompany him to Miami for a rendezvous at the Newport Hotel with Hubbard. Once they got into his room, Hubbard's girlfriend was beaten, raped, and left for dead in a closet.

Bricker shot Hubbard with a pistol, but the gun malfunctioned before he could finish Hubbard off. The Codfish tore the legs off a heavy easy chair and began thrashing the man, upending furniture and breaking lamps. Hubbard still wouldn't die. So Bricker ripped a clothing bar from the wall and crushed the pusher's larynx. His clothes spattered with blood, which also streaked the walls of the room, Bricker ran through the lobby—not for any logical reason but apparently just to stun patrons.

Although both Eggy and Codfish have been charged with the killing, Florida has yet to extradite them.

As far as prosecutors in Pittsburgh were concerned, it didn't matter much. Prosdocimo is not supposed to be released from prison in this lifetime—assuming that Shapp and his appointees on the pardons board never return. Eggy is serving two consecutive life terms, one each for the killings of Sacco and DeStefano.

Eggy had several motives for putting out a $5,000 hit on Sacco, a Dormont thug whose reputation for dealing dope was outdone only by his reputation for consuming more than he sold. Consequently, he owed Eggy $6,000.

More significantly, Sacco's addiction made him reckless. Angry that Prosdocimo wanted payment for the drugs, Sacco on several occasions told Eggy that he had become a police informant and that he was providing detectives with information that would send Prosdocimo to jail. Why he did this was explained with as much thoroughness as why a codfish is ferocious.

Prosdocimo took Sacco's threat seriously. First, he offered Kellington $1,500 to "fuck up" Sacco. But Kellington, who liked the crazy informant, warned him "to watch his step," Kellington later testified.

Sacco couldn't take a hint.

Annoyed that Kellington had done nothing, Prosdocimo turned to Bricker, who in turn decided to subcontract the job for $600 to Miles Gabler, a walkaway from the state's minimum security prison in Greensburg. Gabler was a runt who led something of a doomed career as a miscreant—making him an ideal companion for a guy like Bricker. Gabler had managed to spend most of his adulthood in petty crime, barely eking out a living to support his wife and child.

Although Gabler immediately jumped at the windfall that Bricker offered him in the

Sacco hit, he soon seemed to cool to the idea. Bricker later "told me he didn't think Miles had any balls," Kellington quipped in court.

Ultimately, Bricker helped Gabler make sure the $600 was earned. They asked Sacco to meet them at Butchie's, the Market Square after-hours club which served as the gang's second home, under the pretext that they would give Sacco some wonderful drugs.

Gabler, wearing a hooded shirt, waited outside the bar while Bricker made the connection. As Sacco walked away down the street, Gabler fired a .357 Magnum twice at point-blank range. Bricker looked on with satisfaction, Kellington recalled. Bricker walked up to the warm body to see if Sacco was dead. "He told me Sacco was trying to talk, but there was nothing coming out," Kellington testified.

The Codfish liked to watch things like that up close.

After blowing Melvin Pike off his feet and into eternity with a shotgun blast to the chest in April of 1978, Bricker was said to have returned about an hour later to the Little Washington dance studio where the bloodletting occurred just to see Pike do his last spasms. Instead of holding a shotgun this time, Bricker was licking an ice cream cone.

Pike's number came up because he had become too greedy. The 63-year-old racketeer had too high an opinion of himself. For more than a decade, Pike thrived under the protection of Senator Duffield, who also had befriended Walls, a Pike prodigy.

By early 1978, Pike had so enraged a group of Washington County businessmen with his protection demands that they decided to take up a collection to have him killed, according to investigators. Simultaneously, as Walls later testified, Pike also had upset "No Legs" Hankish, the Wheeling version of a Mafia don. Hankish, a Lebanese immigrant who got his nickname after a bomb blew up at his feet, was furious that Pike was horning in on his gambling operation and siphoning off sports-betting action to the rival gambling network that belonged to Kelly Mannerino, a full-blooded Mafia don who had long controlled vice operations in parts of southwestern Pennsylvania.

Gambling was only one of Hankish's criminal enterprises, as a federal grand jury in 1989 disclosed in a bulky indictment against him and ten associates. Besides overseeing a sports-betting and numbers operation that extended from Rhode Island to Mississippi and from New York to Texas, Hankish also trafficked in stolen merchandise, distributed marijuana and cocaine, engaged in extortion

and blackmail and, of course, put out contracts on uncooperative or otherwise undesir-
able criminals.

He was described as so venal and so lust-
ful that he not only cheated on his income
tax returns, but even used young people to
defraud the West Virginia college student
loan program.

Pike had signed his own death warrant by
getting in the way of such a powerful gangster as Hankish. So it almost was overkill
when Thomas Skelton joined the Get Pike
Club. A slick-haired near-midget who also
developed a chronic Godfather complex,
Skelton never was formally charged in Pike's
slaying. But there was evidence that he provided the impetus for the racketeer's assassi-
nation by kicking in extra cash for the hit.

Skelton ran after-hours joints and a vending machine company with shyster attorney
Allen Frank, who in 1988 was disbarred and
eventually sent to federal prison for perjury.
In 1978, Skelton got wealthy on the poker
machines that Acme Vending Company installed in bars throughout the Mon Valley.

Skelton was described in sworn affidavits
filed by the FBI as having been upset that
Pike was muscling into his own plans to
blanket Washington County with poker machines.

The machines meant a lot to Skelton—

enough to make him want to have McGregor iced for breaking them up during periodic drunken rages, according to Walls and Kellington. Furthermore, the stoolies testified, Skelton had been scared of McGregor ever since McGregor had slapped him around in public—and then told Skelton he'd do the same thing every time he saw him.

Skelton's original lawyer, Raymond Radakovich, a partner of Frank, tried to get his client off the hook in the preliminary hearing by pointing to the testimony of the two informants, who claimed Skelton backed out of the contract after he already had promised $10,000 to Bricker through Kellington. After Skelton lost that round in court, he dropped Radakovich and sought the services of one of the best lawyers money could buy.

He engaged West Virginia's version of Perry Mason, Stanley Preiser, who earlier had presented a brilliant defense of former Allegheny County coroner and commissioner Cyril H. Wecht on fraud charges. Kellington and Walls were no match for the quick-witted Preiser, who resembled a boxer in an elegant pin-stripe suit. As tenacious as he was eloquent, he first persuaded a judge to sever Skelton's case from the other defendants and then proceeded to cast aspersions on every statement that fell from the disreputable informants' lips.

With his aw-shucks Southern accent and down-home demeanor, Preiser sweet-talked the jury into acquitting Skelton.

A few years afterward, Skelton mysteriously disappeared, but not before Preiser got paid.

During Skelton's trial, Preiser adroitly took advantage of Snooky Walls' inflated self-image. He never had the chance in that case to demonstrate any humanitarian qualities.

Walls got that chance in connection with the trials of the Codfish and Eggy for the June 1979 slaying of Gary "Stretch" DeStefano.

For reasons police never fully understood, Walls genuinely liked DeStefano, a 28-year-old Monessen punk whom Walls used as a chauffeur on drug buying and selling trips. He liked him so much that any time he testified about his companion's slaying, Walls cried. Even police were impressed by Walls' feelings for DeStefano. "I think Snooky could accept certain murders as justified, but not Stretch's," said one detective.

DeStefano was the victim of Eggy's greed.

As testimony later showed, Prosdocimo had ordered one hundred eighty-eight pounds of marijuana and ten thousand Quaalude tablets worth about two hundred thousand dollars wholesale from Walls. After the two men showed up at Lester's, a deli

Prosdocimo owned in Squirrel Hill, Eggy told them he didn't have all the cash and asked them to meet him at Butchie's a half hour later.

Once again, Prosdocimo didn't pay for the drugs.

Walls and DeStefano parked their Cadillac and went into Butchie's to meet Prosdocimo, Kellington, and former Pitt football star Bonasorte. Bricker, meanwhile, broke into the Cadillac and was trying to hotwire the car when DeStefano appeared. Before DeStefano could say a word, Bricker pulled out a .22 caliber pistol equipped with a silencer and fired one shot through Stretch's left eye. He then kicked the corpse under a nearby car and telephoned Butchie's, telling Kellington, "The gum band is snapped."

Bricker drove the baby-blue Cadillac to the North Side and transferred the drugs to another car. When he eventually linked up with Kellington and Prosdocimo, Bricker recounted how he killed DeStefano and said how impressed he was that DeStefano died "without a peep." Henceforth, Bricker decided, whenever he shot someone he'd aim for the eyes.

Bricker was acquitted of homicide in DeStefano's killing, and Bonasorte never stood trial. Magistrate Vincent Murovich,

during a preliminary hearing, ruled there
was insufficient evidence against Bonasorte,
although he told the former football ace, "I
suspect you were involved in this." He called
him "reprehensible." Bonasorte had earned
the nickname "Kamikaze Kid" for his aggressive play on the Pitt Panther's specialty
teams between 1973 and 1976.

He showed he hadn't lost that aggressive-
ness when he testified as a defense witness in
Bricker's trial for the Sacco killing. He
mounted the stand and defiantly told the
prosecutor, "This is payback time," going on
to contradict Kellington's testimony by claiming that Monster and Gabler offed Sacco.
When the prosecutor began hammering him
with questions about his alleged drug-dealing
activities, Bonasorte shot his hand into the
air and made a "high five" sign to indicate he
was invoking the Fifth Amendment. After he
finished his testimony, Bonasorte sauntered
off the stand, winked at the prosecutor, and
said, "I'll see you later."

He was still the Kamikaze Kid.

There was a reason for Bonasorte's as-
tounding cockiness. A few weeks earlier, he
had beaten a drug-dealing rap when Common Pleas Judge James R. McGregor ruled
that two undercover detectives fabricated evidence to secure a search warrant they had

used to bust Bonasorte. Although the detectives denied the claim, the ruling meant that prosecutors could not try Bonasorte on the drug charges, even though the raid resulted in the seizure of a cache of downers.

Bonasorte was part of a two-pronged defense strategy that Bricker and Prosdocimo employed in their separate trials for the Sacco hit.

But like much of the rest of the gang's activities, the strategy was diluted by the fact that it required intelligence and savvy to be carried off.

The mistake that both Codfish and Eggy made was thinking that Gabler would, well, think.

Gabler had set the tone for being the surprise defense witness by pleading guilty to first degree murder in the Sacco hit, even though he knew prosecutors were seeking the death penalty. He wanted to prove he had balls. In the topsy-turvy twists that the case took, both Gabler's lawyer and the prosecutor tried to tell the judge that they thought Gabler was lying when he admitted that he fatally shot Sacco.

Standing before Common Pleas Judge Joseph H. Ridge with hands tucked in the back pockets of designer jeans, Gabler said "it didn't really matter" that he was, in effect, putting himself in the electric chair. "I just want to get this off my conscience," he told the judge with a smile of bemusement.

The prosecution showed Ridge that Gabler seemed to have been moved by more than just a guilty conscience. The DA produced records from Western Pen, where Gabler was being housed, that established he had had several visits from an associate of Prosdocimo. Moreover, this associate, who was never identified publicly, had deposited two hundred dollars in Gabler's prison bank account.

Incredible as it seemed that someone would want to go to the electric chair by taking a fall for two hundred dollars, the proceeding became even wilder. Ridge told Gabler that he was not allowed to plead guilty because the prosecution wanted a death sentence. Gabler began arguing, imploring the judge to let him plead guilty to first degree murder so he could pay his debt to society.

Instead of letting Gabler march willingly to the chair, Ridge had him plead guilty to a general charge of homicide. Then the judge imposed a first degree murder conviction after hearing witnesses describe Gabler's role in the Sacco hit.

But the fun and games didn't end there.

Later, Gabler's guilty plea became an embarrassing nuisance for Ridge when it came

time for the judge to decide on a sentence.
Ridge had to decide between life imprisonment and the death penalty. But the judge
didn't want to make the decision by himself.
So Ridge tried to persuade Gabler to em-
panel a jury to determine punishment. He
had sheriff's deputies secretly bring Gabler
to his chambers for a private meeting. When
Gabler refused to let anyone but the judge
decide his fate, Ridge declared that a judge
had the right to involve a jury against the defendant's wishes. That made Gabler and the
prosecutor unlikely allies in a joint appeal of
the ruling.

The state Superior Court sent back the
case with orders that Ridge honor Gabler's
wishes.

Then Gabler declared he didn't kill Sacco,
in effect scotching his own guilty plea and requiring the district attorney's office to seek a
jury trial.

The jury convicted Gabler and sentenced
him to death.

But Gabler will never make it to the electric chair.

When it came time to decide Gabler's
post-trial motions for a reversal of his conviction, Ridge asked two other judges to help
him rule on the appeal. One of the jurists
was McGregor—who had almost testified as

a defense witness for Prosdocimo in the Sacco case. The presiding judge in that trial ruled McGregor could not be put on the witness stand. Exactly what McGregor was to testify about remains a matter of guesswork to this day.

Ultimately, McGregor and Ridge voted against the other panel member, Judge Robert Horgos, and overturned Gabler's death sentence, ordering him to confinement for the rest of his natural life.

The case eventually lost its front-page value even though new trials in some of the homicides took place. Prosecutors gained convictions again, and Gabler, Prosdocimo, Griffen, and Rossi all are serving life sentences.

Codfish Bricker was returned to death row.

As for Kellington and Walls, prison lasted only about five years. They entered the government witness-protection program— getting new identities and new surroundings—because they were convinced that a price remained on their heads.

But there was some suggestion that maybe even the underworld appreciated the service the two informants had provided against such a sloppy and uniformly unsavory group of felons.

Walls left the program two months later and returned to Uniontown, living to testify eventually against Hankish.

Since then, no one has found him worth killing.

▲

# A Collector's Item

## By Abby Mendelson

The Edison Hotel, on Ninth Street near the Allegheny River, is in a part of town where the skirts are short and tight, and nobody asks too many questions.

It's classier than it used to be, now that the bar's been done over, with runner lights, a multicolored dance platform, and a painting of an undraped young lady with a chest, as they say, to *here*. But the marquee still touts girls with names like Tawny and Jewel, and their credentials—their X-rated films—are for serious skin aficionados only.

Dave Goodrich, the night manager, is lanky and well spoken, bespectacled, with mutton chops and long hair hanging out from a black Stoney's Beer cap. Now 44, Goodrich was once a Marine and a writer for Westinghouse. For the last ten years he's been the legendary Doctor of Rock and Roll, the city's most able and thorough entertainment historian.

Born in Venezuela, the son of a Gulf Oil executive, Goodrich moved to Pittsburgh in 1957. A shy 12-year-old, Goodrich didn't fit into his new environment, except in his room with his radio. Back then, rock and roll had a freshness and immediacy that attracted Goodrich. Cribbing nickels out of his lunch money, he bought 45s—little Richard's "Good Golly, Miss Molly" was his first. Goodrich never looked back.

A '60s college drop-out, Goodrich enlisted in the Marines one jump ahead of the draft—and right before the 1968 Tet offensive. After pulling stateside duty as a military publicist, he went back to college and tried his hand at the Great American Novel, an altar at which many hopes have been sacrificed. Later, working at Westinghouse and looking for an outlet, he returned to his first love, music, and began writing concert reviews for the *Pittsburgh Forum* and the *Pittsburgh New Sun*, both of blessed memory.

When a near-marriage broke up, Goodrich figured it was time to change his life. He resigned from Westinghouse and worked on music: attending concerts, writing reviews, composing songs. (A Goodrich-penned novelty number about Anita Bryant made it up the charts to 13 on 96KX.)

Soon after came the gig that set Goodrich firmly in the public eye—and ear. In the late '70s, Don Bombard, with his 13Q Sunday Night Oldies Party, established himself as the city's best, most knowledgeable disc jockey. When Bombard, now heard on New

York's WCBS-FM as Bob Shannon, needed help handling rock trivia, he asked Goodrich to join him. Later, when Bombard said that Goodrich needed a nickname, a station sales rep suggested the Doctor of Rock and Roll—and Goodrich took it seriously. "It added to the responsibility I felt I had to know music," Goodrich says. "I got the title—and then I earned it."

Along with his duties at 13Q, Goodrich also did DJ work of his own at Lou's in Shadyside, and clerked at Lou's Music Connection in Greentree. But tastes and program directors change: the two Lou's closed, Bombard split for New York, and Goodrich dropped out of sight. Later, when his parents died, Goodrich withdrew even farther. "I was in a state of suspended animation," he says.

To fill his days he burrowed deeply into Pittsburgh's past, filling in his own considerable knowledge of local music history. From his Mount Washington apartment, and later from the Edison, he trudged to the library every day, reading microfilms for six hours at a clip—the city's dailies and especially the *Courier*—until his eyes could no longer focus.

The result, in 1985, was the first of a projected comprehensive five-volume Pittsburgh entertainment history. *Key to the City* documented every major Pittsburgh entertain-

ment event from 1928 (when the Stanley
Theater opened) through 1954—movie star
appearances, stage shows, musical acts, and
so on. It also included filmographies of Pittsburghers, anecdotes, and other assorted ef-
fluvia. "I felt I was the only person capable
of documenting the entire history," Goodrich
says. "No other city has a history that complete."

It was exhausting, and now Goodrich admits to working only sporadically on Volume
II. "The bottom line," he says, "is money."
After sales, which ran into the mid-three-
figures, Volume I cost him $5,000.

Aside from his Edison duties, Goodrich
keeps his hand in writing the occasional article. A piece on how the Cultural Trust is
eradicating the indigenous riverside lowlife
was a notable effort, as was a precis of the
rest his history, '54–'79 (the cut-off being the
coming of cable television).

Now creeping into middle age, he's found
himself moving away from rock and roll.
Without his own record collections (Goodrich
has sold more than one over the years when
he's needed money), he doesn't listen to oldies anymore, at least not as played on rigid-
format radio shows. "There's nothing I want
to hear," he laments, and makes a face.

Instead, he's gone South, to the newer,
wide open, country music, writing songs

with darker characters and themes, battered women and teenage runaways. "I'm still as excited about music as I was when I was a kid," Goodrich says. "After all these years, I'm still a fan."

It is an odd, perhaps romantic image, the scholarly historian living inside Pittsburgh's seamiest underlife. "I'm puzzled about why I haven't left here," he admits, then adds, "I'm able to do what I want to do"—write songs and review, attend concerts, work on his book—"and continue to make a contribution to the Pittsburgh music scene."

▲

# The Bare Knuckles Champ

## By Roy McHugh

Joey Diven, everybody says, was the greatest street fighter who ever lived. Frank Deford wrote that in a story for *Sports Illustrated* called "The Boxer and the Blonde." Certainly, Diven was the greatest street fighter who ever lived in Pittsburgh, or, at any rate, the most publicized street fighter. Pittsburgh's last great professional ring fighter, Billy Conn, was the boxer in the title of Frank Deford's story; the blonde was Conn's wife, Mary Louise. Diven, the boxer's friend, appears and reappears as a peripheral character.

At the time Deford heard about Diven, in 1985, Diven's street-fighting days were just a memory. "He's a big, red-faced Irishman," Deford wrote. Red-faced sounds correct, and if you hadn't known Diven in his prime, before the repeated bouts with diabetes, you'd agree that he's big. Diven in his prime—the 1950s and '60s—was more than big. He was massive—six feet three and two hundred eighty-five pounds, firmly upholstered rather than fat, with a nineteen-inch neck between shoulders to match. Diven's brawn was en-

tirely organic, by the way. The only weights
he ever lifted for body-building purposes
were bottles of Iron City beer.

Most good street fighters, wrote Deford in
his *Sports Illustrated* piece, are little guys:
"Big guys grow up figuring nobody will challenge them, so they don't learn how to
fight." Maybe so. For Joey Diven, growing
up in a town where street fighters believe
that the bigger they are the harder they fall,
there were challenges day after day. "He's
like the fastest gun in the West," Billy Conn
used to say. "Somebody's always looking to
try him out."

On a fine autumn evening in 1954, the
University of Pittsburgh football team was
looking to try Joey out. As a direct result,
one first-string linebacker and one first-string
halfback were unable to play against Penn
State the following Saturday, while various
other first-stringers who did play were not at
their best. As another direct result, Pitt lost
the game, 13–0.

A New York City cop, off-duty in Pittsburgh, tried Joey out with a blackjack one
night, and Joey retaliated barehanded. When
they took the cop to Montefiore Hospital, the
physician on duty in the emergency room
kept shaking his head and asking, "What was
he hit with?" No fist, the doctor insisted,
could do so much damage.

There was also the time that Joey and one associate, having heard that they were wanted inside to be tried out, kicked down the door of a social resort called the St. Lorenzo Club. Within fifteen minutes, the St. Lorenzo Club was in much the same condition as Stalingrad after World War II. Joey, no braggart, refused to take credit for a triumph against overwhelming odds, pointing out that not all of the club members had been casualties.

"A lot of them," he explained with a finicky concern for exactitude, "ran."

They knew that while violence was repugnant to Joey—"I've never picked a fight in my life; I've never sucker-punched anyone," he has said—his repugnance disappeared in the heat of combat. "Once I get started," Joey admitted back then, "I'm like an earthquake."

The image was imprecise. In reality, Joey fought with a certain stateliness, delivering powerful left hooks and straight rights in the approved, classic textbook fashion. He was not wildly aggressive. But with one hand Joey could grab a two-hundred-pound adversary, and in the words of Billy Conn's brother, the late Jackie Conn, "crush him unconscious." His other great advantage was that when celebrated punchers took their best shots at Joey, landing with full effect, he

appeared not to notice. This had a tendency
to make celebrated punchers lose their bel-
ligerence.

Left to his own inclinations, Joey brimmed
over with good will, and still does. His personality attracts rather than intimidates. In
his youth, he had the face of an oversized
cherub. His smile, which never has changed,
was ingratiating. In short, Joey Diven can be
a crowd pleaser, as the Democratic party machine learned to its embarrassment thirty
years ago when Joey lived in Oakland and
ran for the office of constable. Underestimat-
ing his popularity, the ward bosses opposed
him. There appeared to be no way that Joey
could win. And then one day as the primary
election drew near, a parade wound through
Oakland that tied up traffic for blocks
around. The parade was for Joey Diven. He
defeated the organization's man by one hundred forty votes. The general election in November, with the party machine now behind
him, was a Diven landslide.

Toots Shor called from New York to con-
gratulate Joey that night. Shor felt indebted
to Joey for services rendered as a keeper of
the peace. On one notable occasion, a large,
drunken, obstreperous Texan was making a
pest of himself in Shor's restaurant, picking
fights with the other customers. Swiftly and
efficiently, Joey put an end to the unpleas-

antness. First the Texan and then his Stetson flew out the door, with Joey calling after him, "Don't forget your hat."

Joey from then on was something of a personage in Shor's. His knack for sociability didn't hurt. Among the illustrious in many walks of life, Joey Diven always had friends. For years when Frank Leahy was coaching, Joey popped up on the Notre Dame bench— Leahy's guest—at football games from South Bend to Los Angeles. The World Series ring Joey wears was the gift of a major-league umpire, Jocko Conlan. And for a night on the town during one of his visits to New York, Joey's transportation was a chauffeured Rolls Royce that belonged to the Duke himself, John Wayne.

Toots Shor's was the place where Joey mingled easily with the elite of the sporting and theatrical worlds. It was possible to meet almost anybody in Shor's. If they were friends of the owner, they were friends of Joey. He was there one night with two Pittsburgh pals—Bob Prince, the late Pirates' announcer, and George Katsos, a part-time artist and bartender—when Ernest Hemingway walked in. "Ernest!" cried Katsos, recognizing him from his pictures. Ernest, it was clear, was in a jovial mood. "He came over to me like he knew me," Katsos said later on. Launching a brief, though beautiful, friend-

ship, they threw their arms around one
another, and Hemingway joined the group
at the bar, which now included a baseball
player, Hank Sauer. After Katsos had taken
care of the formal introductions, Hemingway
ordered drinks. He stood there chatting genially. Fifteen minutes passed; Hemingway
seemed to be having a good time. Finally Diven drew Katsos aside. "Prince keeps asking
me if you really know that guy with the
beard, that Hemingway," Joey said. "Who
the hell is he?"

With politicians, Joey was more in his element. In 1960, running for president, John
F. Kennedy came to Pittsburgh and gave a
speech at the Syria Mosque. Joey, not even a
constable then, listened serenely from the
dais, where he sat in the front row with such
privileged Pennsylvania Democrats as Governor David L. Lawrence and Senator Joseph
S. Clark. Governor Lawrence and Senator
Clark had earned the right to be on the dais
through long years of seniority as elected
public officials. Joey Diven had earned it in
five minutes of conversation with Senator
Clark's wife.

Approaching her as a stranger, he had said
that both Kennedy and her husband had his
support and that Allegheny County was safe
for the Democrats. Mrs. Clark seemed de-
lighted to hear it. They were up on the
stage—the program was about to begin—and

she suggested to Joey, "Please take this chair
next to mine." His only regret about accept-
ing her invitation was a minor one: "All the
roaches from Oakland"—Joey's term for that
old gang of his—"kept yelling, 'Whaddaya
doin' up there?' "

Advancing in political favor, Joey was a
county detective when, in 1962, Kennedy
visited Pittsburgh as president. The Secret
Service needed help with security, and Joey
had volunteered. He was thus in position, on
Kennedy's arrival from the airport, to offer
him a personal welcome as he stepped from
his limousine.

"You're doing a great job, Prez, and we're
praying for you," Joey said, grasping Kennedy's hand.

The roaches from Oakland were silent for
once. Appearances to the contrary, Joey had
their respect as protector and patron. For
roaches who were down and out, he would
sometimes    hold    benefit    raffles—raffles
with no prizes awarded. As a constable, he
refused to serve process papers, allowing
his four deputies—one-time down-and-out
roaches—to collect all the fees. And the deputies had instructions from Joey never to
evict a tenant behind in the rent. "I come
from a poor street myself," Joey would say.

It was in the role of protector that Joey
made his stand against the 1954 Pitt football
team. An Oakland roach had been slugged by

a Pitt co-captain, and Joey at once intervened. The maxim, "Joey Diven's so tender-hearted he wouldn't harm a fly—and don't ever let him catch *you* harming a fly or he'll bash your brains in," also applied where roaches were concerned. He did not bash in the brains of the football player, but rather mauled him with one hand while bending him, with the other hand, over the hood of a parked car. The hand Joey was using as a fulcrum—his left—had nine stitches in it from a previous fight.

As the football player struggled to break loose, reinforcements arrived from the nearby Pitt campus. Then at intervals for the next half-hour, the beleaguered player's teammates kept flinging themselves at Joey. They scrimmaged up Bouquet Street from Forbes to Fifth Avenue, where Joey's undamaged right put the team's most valuable short-yardage threat into a hedge row. In the alley behind the old Strand Theater, Joey braced himself with his back to the wall and fought off a rush that would have sacked any quarterback in the country. At last, giving up, his assailants withdrew. The White Knight of Oakland—Joey's nickname forever afterward—had routed them. All by himself.

Joey was now the symbol of Oakland's resistance to the university's encroachment on neighboring real estate. More in answer to

duty's call than in anger, he continued to ter-
rorize the Pitt football players, often with
both hands. Meanwhile, a national crisis had
developed. Bookmakers from coast to coast
were beginning to grow suspicious of Pitt
games. In the face of the team's unpredict-
ability, the Minneapolis odds line—Las Vegas
had not yet taken over—no longer seemed
trustworthy. Drastic action was called for,
and the man who set the national betting
odds went straight to the root of the trouble.
He placed a special observer in Oakland with
instructions to notify him by telephone
whenever a Pitt football player was rash
enough to cross Joey's path.

Desperate, Coach John Michelosen declared the more perilous sections of Oakland
off-limits to his squad. But for Joey, hostility
was a burden. He called on Michelosen offi-
cially and they worked out the terms of an
armistice. Peaceful co-existence became the
watchword, although for kicks one night Joey
turned over a telephone booth with a former
Pitt end trapped inside, glass walls on three
sides of him and the door against the floor.

The relationship between Diven and
Yutzie Pasquarelli, a street-corner news ven-
dor as strongly pro-Pitt as Joey was pro-Notre
Dame, was somewhat special. In the 1930s,
Yutzie had been a student at Pitt, selling pa-
pers until late at night and going to class in

the mornings. There came a day when his economics professor said to him, "Look here, I can't have you falling asleep in my class all the time. You snore. I see you at night selling papers. How much do you make on that job?" Yutzie's answer—$125 a week— widened the professor's eyes. The holder of two degrees, he was making—in those Depression days—about $35 a week on his own job. "Take my advice as an economics professor and get out of school," he said to Yutzie, who wasted no time in doing so. He added to his wealth by selling papers in the daytime as well as at night, and was able to lend money to impecunious Pitt football players, interest free. All he asked in return was a place on the Pitt bench at home games. Joey Diven, meanwhile, was sitting on Notre Dame's bench, and when the Notre Dame-Pitt game was over, they would each cross the field and meet to shake hands. "Like the coaches do," Joey pointed out.

As legendary in Oakland as the war between Joey and Pitt was his encounter with a subdivision of the New York City police force. The Ancient Order of Hibernians, a fraternal organization known for brevity's sake as the Irish Club, had a second-floor barroom in Oakland where Joey helped out as the semi-official bouncer and where everybody went to relax on the weekend of a big

police convention. Informality was the key-
note, and Joey, whose relations with the
Pittsburgh police were excellent, addressed a
flippant remark to an inspector of his acquaintance. A New York patrolman, overhearing it, rebuked him. Joey's answer was
another flippant remark. Again the New
Yorker rebuked him, adding, for better em-
phasis, a sharp blow to the head with a blackjack.

Eyewitnesses recall that a look of extreme
annoyance flickered across Joey's face. This
and a rivulet of blood were the only indica-
tions that he had been hit. Joey invited the
cop to the parking lot, took another rap from
his blackjack, and disarmed him. Three
punches later, it was necessary to summon an
ambulance for the cop.

Subsequently, Joey was busily occupied in
bouncing other New York policemen off the
cars that were parked in the lot. A squad of
Pittsburgh police, including Joey's two older
brothers, appeared on the scene and at
length got him into a paddy wagon. When
the paddy wagon stopped shaking, they knew
it was safe to release him. No charges were
pressed.

The storming of the St. Lorenzo Club by
Joey and another Oakland street fighter,
Jimmy Newell, was also of interest to the po-
lice. By the time the police got there, a club

member called Bully was running for his life, with Joey in thunderous pursuit. Joey caught up with Bully, and the police caught up with the two of them, on someone's front porch, where Joey surrendered amiably after one cop attracted his attention by cracking him on the head with a nightstick.

Like their father before them, Joey's brothers, Bobby and Bernie, were beat cops. In their youth, the three Divens invented a game called One Punch. It was simple to play. One brother would punch the other as hard as he could and then the other, if able, would punch back. The last time they played it was when Bernie, taking his turn against Joey, threw what he believed to be the hardest right hand of his life. On that point, alas, there was no direct evidence, for Joey, breaking the rules, stepped to one side, and a storefront window took the impact of Bernie's punch. Afterward Joey laughed about it and Bernie himself was in stitches—seventy-five stitches by actual count.

Once on a question of public safety, the Pittsburgh Police Department grudgingly deferred to Joey. With the streets of the city under two feet of snow, Superintendent Lawrence Maloney had called off the annual St. Patrick's Day parade, bitterly disappointing a large crowd of Hibernians assembled at the takeoff point, a saloon. "The Superintendent says we're not marching," shouted Joey. "How about it?"

They marched, with the Superintendent leading. "If you can't lick 'em, join 'em," he muttered.

St. Patrick's Day was the one day in the year when Joey turned militant. Working the front door at the Irish Club on a never-to-be-forgotten St. Patrick's Day night, he confronted three strangers wearing bright orange ties. "That's like a mockery," Joey growled. The upshot of it was that the strangers made a trip to the hospital. "I punched the one and threw the other two down the stairs," Joey recalls.

At Pete Coyne's in Oakland, a saloon with a neon shamrock above the entrance, run-of-the-bar St. Patrick's Day fights went virtually unnoticed, but on one occasion a fight broke out that compared in ferocity with the Battle of the Boyne. Joey, seizing each of the two instigators by the scruff of the neck, delivered a stern lecture on thoughtlessness. "This is Pete's big day," he reminded them. "He can make a buck and you're spoiling it."

With that, Joey hurled them through the plate-glass front door, which happened to be closed.

In the 1950s and '60s, Joey spent most of his leisure hours in small Irish bars such as Coyne's. Tears filled the eyes of the old Irish couples in the booths at the Oakland Cafe when Joey sang "Galway Bay." Jackie Conn, envious, attempted to drown him out one night but was silenced almost instantly when a large, heavy, rectangular object descended with stunning force on his head. Jackie liked to tell how surprised he was, declaring in astonishment, "A little old lady whacked me with her purse."

Little old ladies were partial to Joey, and vice versa. Friends of his, driving through Oakland, were apt to be whistled down. "See that lady on the corner, waiting for a bus?" Joey would say. "Take her wherever she's going." Younger ladies were partial to Joey for his smile and his wavy brown hair. Married now to the former Barbara Long, he has two grown sons as big as he is.

Dignified and status-minded, he cuts a benign figure at his own bar in Oakland, Philip D's, named for his nephew and partner, Phil Diulus. There are seldom any fights. No longer do challengers walk up to Joey, a balding man of sixty, and introduce themselves with a punch. In Pete Coyne's and the Irish Club and the Oakland Cafe, this sort of thing was commonplace. Joey thought nothing of it. As he told writer Frank Deford, "It wasn't ever vicious. In those days, nobody ever drew guns or knives or used clubs. Nobody was loco with drugs. And it never took more than four or five minutes. Somebody would get in one good shot, and that would wear you out pretty quick, and after that there'd be a lot of mauling and rassling, and then it was history. As soon as a guy said he'd had enough, that was it. You'd buy each other a drink and maybe end up getting fractured together."

To be sure, it was never Joey who said that he'd had enough. And when Joey got carried away, he tended to disregard the code. In the Oakland Cafe once, a challenger walked up and punched Joey and then reconsidered.

"Uh . . . I made a mistake," he said.

"You sure did," Joey informed him, underlining those words with a short, purposeful movement of his left hand.

"That was one time I thought Joey'd killed somebody," Jackie Conn would reminisce when the subject came up.

Offering to be Joey's manager, Billy Conn urged him to turn pro. Conn arranged for a fight between Joey and Nate Smith, a long, lean, heavyweight who found his true calling in the 1960s as a civil-rights activist and labor leader. Because of Joey's drawing power in Oakland, the promoter agreed to pay him six hundred dollars, unheard of for a four-round preliminary. Tempted, Joey at first was willing. He no more than half-listened when Billy Neumont, a lightweight once managed by Conn, advised him to forget the whole thing. "Joey," said Neumont earnestly, "this ain't the same as a street fight, believe me. Nate Smith will run for three rounds and in the fourth round you'll drop from exhaustion. Then those roaches from Oakland will boo you right out of the arena." Billy Conn was more reassuring. "He told me that Nate Smith had tuberculosis," said Joey.

But neither Billy's encouragement nor the prospect of sudden riches could get Joey into a gym. He believed in and practiced gracious living, a full-time occupation that left him no margin for training. And so Joey never did fight Nate Smith. There was one final reason: "My widowed mother, God bless her, said, 'Joey—don't.' "

His future, he decided, was in politics. In that particular ring, he had rolled with the punches for years. Administrative assistant to County Commissioner Tom Foerster for the better part of a decade now, Joey always has an employer. In the late 1970s it was Pete Joyce, the prothonotary. "What the hell's a prothonotary?" President Harry Truman wanted to know on a memorable guided tour of the City-County Building. A prothonotary, as only Pittsburghers, and not many of those, are aware, is a sort of glorified notary public with a large staff of record keepers and certain patronage jobs to dispense. One such job involving no paper work was Joey Diven's for five or six years. In any case, whoever his boss—prothonotary, county commissioner, mayor, district attorney, or what have you—Joey campaigns for him loyally, sometimes backing winners and sometimes backing losers, either sharing in the spoils or holding an empty bag. Only once has he run for high office himself, and the office, as it happens, was prothonotary. He ran against Pete Joyce, the long-time incumbent, who had fired Diven the year before when there were payroll cuts.

Joey Diven, everybody says, was the greatest street fighter who ever lived. He was not, nor did he expect to be, the greatest office seeker. When the final returns came in—Pete Joyce defeated him by twenty thousand votes—Joey laughed.

"What the hell's a prothonotary?" he shouted.

▲

# A Brush with Class

# By Abby Mendelson

Rain falls on the skylight of Bob Qualters' art studio, and barren tree branches sway overhead. The heater's on in the made-over Tilbury Street garage, and Qualters, a bearish man with graying hair, wears a brown sweater and corduroys. It's a mere nine months before a new show and he's fussing unmercifully.

He has three oils so far, softer, less busy than the bustling, heavily detailed cityscapes he has sold in the past. In one, a man lies on his back in the park and gazes into the blue night sky. In the second, people stop on the Panther Hollow bridge and look at houses rising from the soft green South Oakland hills. In the third, fog burns off the Mon River and leaves Downtown a smoldering orange in the early morning light.

Although clearly grounded in the city—Qualters' lifelong subject—these paintings are studies in primary colors and the artist's persona as much as views of Pittsburgh. Gone is much of the sharp detail—the bricks, mills, luncheonette bric-a-brac—captured in his earlier works. Gone, too, are the odd scraps of text around the edges—reflections and poetry and quotations that were his trademark. "It seemed a bit pretentious," Qualters shrugs. "A little artificial."

If anything, the words have retreated inside. The night dreamer, for instance, is surrounded by disquieting thoughts in red, while two human figures loom over him like parents intruding on wayward thinking. The green vista is soft and dreamlike, a medieval romance. The orange city rises from the mist of history, from the anvil of time.

Qualters' other Pittsburgh was a crowded place, full of people and action, lines and angles, contrasts and words. Arguably, those paintings captured Pittsburgh better than any other, from its darkest moments, on a rain-swept Second Avenue night, to its lightest, as seasons changed on the hills and river valleys.

Born in McKeesport fifty-five years ago, the son of a real estate appraiser and grandson of a man who worked in National Tube, Qualters attended Carnegie Tech, pulled a hitch in the army, split for San Francisco, taught in the Catskills, and finally returned for good in 1968. "I always wanted to come back," he says. "I knew Pittsburgh was where I was supposed to be." A pause. "Something about this place is important to me."

"There's a tendency to apologize for staying home," Qualters adds, "and I used to think of that as a failure of nerve. But it just felt right. If I had my choice, I'd never live anywhere else.

"Your sense of form, your sense of rightness, come from your earliest memories," he says. "Pittsburgh *looks* right. Dramatic. Full of contrast, atmosphere. When I was a kid it was dark and spooky—massive and theatrical. It was my earliest understanding of space and light and color."

Qualters for the last fifteen years has made his living primarily as an artist—in good times and bad. And there were plenty of bad. "Pittsburgh as a subject was seen as gauche," he recalls, "ordinary." Such criticism might have hurt, but he never quit. "I never really considered anything else," he says. So he painted, and painted what he wanted—the city that felt so right, the ordinary places that all of us have seen, brief glimpses during daily routines. Downtown streets from coffee shop windows. Schenley Park. The Jenkins Arcade.

Qualters sells at various galleries, does commissions and an occasional mural. "Right now I'm selling well." Qualters shrugs. "That'll change."

He's in the studio by eight in the morning, chewing a toothpick and chain drinking decaf. He'll break for lunch and a walk, then hit the canvas again. "My tendency is to overwork," Qualters admits.

At one time he used photos to get his city just so. Now he's switched to memory, letting it distort, letting it dictate what's important. "Painting should reflect the moment you get the idea," he says. "I wanted that feeling from my own experience, and I wanted it as directly as possible," capturing that *gestalt*, the moment it all hits.

Not that he hasn't gone the other way. He's tried big-theme works, such as series about Rilke poems. And heavy ideas slipped into a piece about the Penn Station rotunda, which became a kind of Orpheus ascending from the underworld. The technique is there, but the Qualters warmth and wit are missing. "It looks like it wants to be about something important," he criticizes. "But it's not."

If these were false steps, they are only evidence of Qualters' desire to keep challenging himself. For this next show, he's turned again, to simpler images and more personal themes, stronger primary colors, paper (as opposed to canvas) because it's more spontaneous, more direct. The latest trio is simpler, cleaner, the product of a man more at peace with himself and his landscape. "These new paintings feel like they're after something different," he says. "They feel like something I wanted to do."

Still, he's not happy. The orange city is

fine, but the fog looks like steamy sunlight, and Qualters is trying to fix it. He masks the picture with brown paper, then with his hands, muttering that the fog isn't opaque like fog. "It's one of those paintings that's supposed to be easy," he grumps. "It never works out that way."

Qualters blocks out a part of the South Side with his hands, then shakes his head. "It's too early for this series," he says. "I'll have to see what happens."

▲

# Extreme Circumstances

## By Jack Graphic

This particular tussle between a bad ass and a tough cop ended with the traditional Pittsburgh Bureau of Police *thwaaaap* upside the head, a crisp crunchy noise followed by the collapse of rubbery knees. The woozy conclusion might have been ordinary, but the crime was far from average, the criminal was not your normal mugger, and the lawman wasn't cut from the standard mold.

For instance, when the thwaaaapee hit the deck, the advice he heard was not remotely referenced on the Miranda warning card: "Matter of fact, tonight you are a guest of the city. Move one muscle and you're going to the hospital in a coma, you toe-sucking sonovabitch."

Jeep Toler, the vigilant vice detective, had just clamped shut his single-handed dragnet around Lamont Lampkin, a pervert who charted new waters for behavioral science enthusiasts.

Lest we forget the reason for all the ruckus:

The fat black lady at the Uptown bus stop lay stretched out, face up, one shoulder propped against the carpet-and-tile discount store. Her torso was balanced on an elbow, her upper lip was oozing from the gash, her lungs were pumping out agonized moans, her trenchcoat was ripped, her grocery bag was shredded, and the contents were askew on the pavement. She clutched the strap of her purse, but no longer was a purse connected to it. Her household budget was ruined. Her world was confused, distorted. Her heart was thumping furiously. Her eyes were bulging, and her left foot was sopping wet with slobber.

One high-heeled shoe was gone.

"Did he suck your toes, ma'am? Was it the toe-sucker who did this?" Jeep implored, his Irish tenor raised to clear fog from her brain.

He had noticed the missing shoe as soon as he stepped out of the unmarked patrol car.

Jeep *knew* this MO.

The maniac Jeep was after had a compulsion, an irresistible urge, an uncontrollable fascination. He got extremely aroused by female extremities—his was a fetish for fetid feet, as it were. He achieved a sordid satisfaction by sucking women's five little piggies—the ones who went to market, the ones who stayed home, the ones who ate roast beef, the ones who had none—into his mouth all at once. There is no other layman's way to put it. The answer to *why* Lamont Lampkin chose this kind of life—or was driven to it—will remain a matter of grave concern, perhaps of government-funded study, for specialists in aberrant social conduct for maybe a millennium. The motive is not important here, just that he did it.

"Oooooolllllooord in the heaven! Ooooaall-llmighty! Help me, it hurts sooo baaad!" wailed the disoriented victim, her many sources of pain manifesting themselves in the contortions of her sweaty face.

On his haunches, Jeep leaned closer to the woman and asked again—using other words, but still beseeching, trying to divert her concentration from the suffering, to penetrate that cloud of mental chaos. "Police, ma'am. Ambulance is on the way, ma'am." In those days—1976—an ambulance meant a paddy-wagon with an oxygen tank that had a busted pressure gauge, plus there was a versatile cot which came in handy for transporting unconscious drunks, for delivering babies, for emergencies like the fat black lady's, or for catching an hour of z-time while an officer's partner stood watch, either driving around or idling the motor in an alley. Nobody bitched much about it in those days, because when a cop was needed, a cop usually was there. Cops chased after thugs back then, too, rather than wait for their mugshots to flash across the screen weeks later on *Crimestoppers* or *America's Most Wanted,* the TV programs that have replaced old-fashioned flatfoot dirtywork. Like the type Jeep did.

"What did he look like, ma'am? What was he wearing? Which way did he go?" Jeep was shouting, as detached as he could be, like the manual said, but full of adrenaline. He never had gotten this close to the toe-sucker. Every second—although wasted patiently, compassionately—translated into another step toward another escape for the toe-sucker. Jeep wanted the confrontation this very night, but the chance was slipping, slipping, slipping.

"Lavender, lavender—everything is lavender," she whispered.

Was this delirium? A tiny clue? A breakthrough? "What is lavender, ma'am?" He grasped her forearm.

"Everything, I said, dammit—his jacket, his pants, his socks, his hat. And I ain't crazy, neither, 'cause—"

"I know you're not crazy, ma'am. Which way did he go?" Jeep could not afford to let her drift onto a tangent.

"If you shut up with the questions, I'll tell you which way did he go—he didn't go no way. He's standin' right over there—and that's my shoe!" She aimed her accusation at

Lamont Lampkin, who was among a dozen or so spectators not twenty yards away in the lot of an abandoned gas station. In his armpit was tucked a high-heeled shoe, and there was no reasonable doubt it would match perfectly the one on the fat black lady's right foot. This Prince Charming was jiving—inconspicuously, he probably thought—with the onlookers. He was not actively searching for any Miss Cinderella, although his attire suggested some sort of fairy tale.

Jeep whirled and yelled "Hey, you!" in the general direction of the bystanders, and—guess what—only prime suspect Lamont Lampkin responded.

"Who, me? I didn't do nuthin, man; this is a p-r-o-fessional frame job, Jack," he protested when Jeep approached at a determined trot. The crowd parted, and Lamont Lampkin retreated, shuffling backward initially, then turning to run. In the process, he continued with his alibi, indignantly:

"I found this, man—I came to give it back to the old lady. Some other dude whopped her, man. You can't arr-"

*Thwaaaap!*

Jeep attempted to sheathe his service revolver—never to be used as a club, according to regulations, but a good noggin cracker nonetheless. It wouldn't slide back into the holster. He tried again, a practiced movement not requiring an experienced cop to avert his sight from the slumped prisoner. Again, the gun wouldn't fit into the slot in the leather. Jeep gawked at the sidearm—the barrel was shaped like a banana, all four inches of the blued steel. Jeep jammed it into the waistline of his trousers. "Matter of fact"—Jeep started all antagonistic communications with that phrase—"tonight . . . "

Jeep was upset—he knew he would have to pay the department for a new revolver. As for the arrest, he was ecstatic. For that he would get overtime—an even trade.

For several evenings Jeep had cruised the lower Hill, the Bluff, and Uptown—where the toe-sucker had struck many times before. When the radio broadcast sent a wagon crew to assist "the woman down" at the bus stop, Jeep was a block away. He arrived ahead of the first squad car. Minutes later, the crime was solved, the victim was reunited with her shoe, and the menacing predator was under wraps.

Or so it seemed.

Everybody forgot one thing—the *Constitution*, man.

Lamont Lampkin's public defender on the day of the trial—eight months and two postponements later—raised a helluva legal technical stink outside the courtroom.

At issue was the fat black lady's groggy state of mind at the moment she positively identified Lamont Lampkin from twenty yards away. In her more stable condition eight months and two postponements later, she wasn't so sure—especially after thinking everything over while seated next to Lamont Lampkin in the witness room at the Courthouse. He was wearing a dull gray suit, white shirt, and a necktie.

To counter this brilliant lawyering, the rookie assistant district attorney waved around Lamont Lampkin's three-page rap sheet, threatening to introduce as evidence all those prior convictions on stickup charges.

The prosecutor's adversary overcame that maneuver with an eloquent rebuttal:

"Go ahead, and I'll grill you and that monster cop down the street in federal court where they love brutality cases."

Jeep smelled it coming, a different version of the Mexican standoff. A plea bargain was in the making.

Lamont Lampkin walked from the Courthouse that day as a negotiated probationer, having promised sincerely to perform community service as punishment. The probation office found a cooperative hospital willing to help rehabilitate him as an orderly.

Imagine the thousands of bare tootsies that

Lamont Lampkin said no-no-no to when they tempted him from under the covers.

*   *   *

That was not to be Jeep Toler's first or final insult.

One day while nonchalantly passing through the cellblock in the old Public Safety Building—the corridor also was known as the bullpen—a hand reached through the iron bars and grabbed Jeep's throat. It was some guy whom Jeep had nabbed years earlier and forgotten about. Jeep, choking, reached in and grabbed the guy's throat. It was another of those Mexican standoffs until Jeep noticed the hand gripping one of the bars for leverage. Jeep took a pacifier from his back pocket—a slapstick, a miniature billyclub—and whacked the knuckles as hard as he could. The accoster melted. Jeep had chopped off an index finger. Eventually, Jeep was defending himself down the street in federal court where they loved brutality cases. Jeep lost the lawsuit and was assessed damages of $3,000. As he and the plaintiff sneered at each other on the way out, Jeep told the winner: "Matter of fact, I'd rather lose $3,000 than never be able to do this," and with that Jeep plunged his own index finger up his own nose. When he withdrew it, he wiggled the slimy point at the guy. Courtroom decorum never was a priority with Jeep, but getting the last laugh was.

* * *

Like the time Jeep headed down Forbes Avenue toward Market Square one morning in the wee hours. He was going to get a beer before the saloons closed. He had just turned in the car keys at the end of his shift and was walking with a carnation he bought earlier for his mother from a street vendor.

Three hooligans, fresh from a motorcycle foray somewhere, surrounded Jeep and made derisive comments about the flower. One thing led to another and finally the trio decided to relieve Jeep of the carnation, and his wallet. One of them had a knife, but none knew Jeep carried a badge and a gun. Jeep, feigning that he was afraid, pretended to reach for his wallet to accommodate the fellas. He instead produced ole Roscoe and promptly triggered the equalizer six times. One bullet scored, piercing the kneecap of the knife-toter. The other two fled, unscathed, but absolutely amazed. It was really loud!

When the medics were lifting the wounded troublemaker into the back of the ambulance, Jeep saw him whimpering. Jeep squeezed the kneecap—which certainly caused a memorable sensation—and informed the patient: "Matter of fact, the next time you hang out with your buddies, when the wind blows, your leg is going to sound like this," and with that, Jeep whistled through his teeth.

▲

# Blacks and Whites and Grays

By Abby Mendelson

It's a crisp morning in Mark Perrott's South Side studio, a spare, white, Bingham Street room. Perrott, in plaid shirt and jeans, has just come off the road, from a three-day shoot at a National Steel plant in Detroit, and, as he puts it, is emptying the bag.

"I could have done better," he groans. "I could have been more clever. I could have brought better lights." Mercifully, the storm passes quickly.

Now 43, a Beaver native and son of a Westinghouse executive, Perrott got into photography at age 11, when an uncle left him an old Mercury half-frame, a camera that yielded seventy-two prints from a thirty-six-exposure roll. He shot friends, motorcycles, hoodlums—the world. "I loved that camera," Perrott recalls. "What a gas!"

He attended Allegheny College, and later Carnegie Mellon, with an eye to teaching photography. About twenty years ago he got sidetracked shooting, "making stuff," Perrott says, "earning a living. That's the way it's gone ever since, making images of what other people make first. That's okay. That's an okay challenge."

But okay isn't enough, not for Perrott, a man who thrives on tension, on trying to stuff too much into an impossible schedule, on artistic challenges. "It's tough juggling making a living and personal projects," he admits. "They are exclusive, and it's hard for me, especially giving myself permission to do my own work. In my bag, guilt is crushing. But I'm itchy when I don't have anything going. So there's always three projects holding for me," Perrott adds. "There's always too much. They're what keep me reasonably stable."

Although much of his corporate work is color, for his own projects Perrott prefers black-and-white. "That's my thing," he nods. "Black-and-white pushes me to confront issues other than the surface, other than the *look*. My stuff hasn't said 'color' to me. So I've never moved on."

Perrott has exhibited in Pittsburgh and New York, with work in museum collections here and in San Francisco. His memorable, quirky shows have included *Tattoo Witness*, *Eliza* (an essay, subsequently made into a book, on the abandoned J&L mill prior to its demolition), and one that combined mother's and daughter's faces in single, stitched-together images. His forthcoming show is a daring work that is as much about the artifice of photography as the classics it depicts: The Landscape, The Nude, Special Effects, and so on.

But there's a catch. Intruding, re-directing each picture, are the impedimenta of photography: lights, wires, and a bulky old Speedgraphic mounted on a tripod. (Perrott shot the actual photos with his Hasselblad.) "I love photography as a way of having a presence in the world without my being there," Perrott says. "But the camera can really be a pain. All that stuff we bring—how intrusive we are. We get in the way. Unwittingly, sometimes, but we get in the way. So these turned out to be more autobiographic than I had wanted.

"The working title was *What Gets Light*," Perrott adds. "Maybe it should be 'who gets lucky'—in life or light. Because what happens to get in the frame sometimes just happens. And what happens to get in the frame of my life sometimes just happens."

The first photo is the prow of an abandoned lifeboat beached beneath the Fort Pitt Bridge. "A lifeboat," Perrott says. "I'm still looking for my own."

"Sentimental Journey" is a B-29, shot and lit much like his father's war souvenir at home.

"The Nude" has four lights, one camera, one female torso—and took three days of shooting.

"Packing Peanuts" is Perrott's F/X photo, "the snow that Fred Astaire dances in," he says. The shapes twist and fall, some illuminated, some translucent in the light's glare. Shot at 1/500th of a second, the pattern is random, frozen in air. "There's a lot of happy accident," he says.

"Dorothy," the Duquesne Works on Route 835, sits vacant beneath a glowering, dusky sky. In the foreground are an empty Stroh's bottle, an abandoned tire, and an open auto trunk. It's a powerful scene, dead and dying.

Perrott found nature in the Laurel Highlands, in a small glade near a pond. He took rolls of standard woods shots, mist off the pond, leafy reflections, golden sunlight. It was all very nice, all very boring. "Perrott," he told himself, "get into it. Nature Photography!"

Through these and other Perrott photos, the heavy light and shadow, the strong lines seem indelibly to be a part of his city. And for good reason, Perrott says. "Pittsburgh is a wonderfully ironic city, and I love it visually: grit and grime against the glitter. That quality means that the city never seems to have a settled face. It always has a surprise. So I've never, ever, thought of leaving. Pittsburgh has just enough of everything for me."

Except artistic support, perhaps. Perrott admits that for all their skill and poignancy, his shows have never made money. "Not a penny," he says. "I am blessed if I'm close to even. But I don't care about that. Because I am incredibly happy in the middle of doing the work—there, involved with the camera. The legacy of that—the exhibition, the prints—is nice, but physically and emotionally doing the work is the most exquisite thing for me. Whatever I get back, I get back. The pictures don't need payback, and I don't either."

▲

# A Rose among Thorns

## By Adrian McCoy

In the peak hours of the Downtown lunchtime feeding frenzy, strains of classical flute weave through the drone of the wheels of commerce.

Outside the back door of G. C. Murphy's is the last place one would expect to hear a live performance of the "Adagio" from Mozart's G Major Concerto, or Bach's Suite in B Minor. The playing is pure, sweet, and the audience doesn't buy tickets or wear tuxes.

It comes from street musician Betty Labas, who for the past five years has brought a unique color to the Downtown landscape. Betty gets a warm reception from the lunch crowd. Although she doesn't solicit funds, people make a point of dropping change in the instrument case, or stopping by to talk.

Betty is partially sighted, and gets around with the help of a guide dog, Hershey. But sight problems don't stop her from getting Downtown to play, or from writing fiction and poetry.

Born in 1936 and raised in Pittsburgh, she started training at age ten with Alois Hrabak, who taught music in the Pittsburgh Public Schools. She played in the All City Orchestra through her school years. In 1959, she joined The Pittsburgh Youth Symphony.

A violinist named Lorin Maezel was there then, too.

Pittsburgh Symphony Orchestra principal flutist Bernard Goldberg once asked Betty if she wanted to study with him. She regretfully turned down the opportunity, thinking she'd be betraying her beloved mentor Hrabak. She later told him about it. "Dumkopf!" Hrabak replied.

Her musical career—the first one—was short-lived: she never got to play a concert with Youth Symphony.

Her husband was out of work, and she ended up having to sell the flute.

Like many other women of that time, Betty gave up thoughts of a career and became a full-time mother and wife.

Four kids, eleven years, and a divorce later, she went back to music, even if it meant finding her own stage. Taking a cue from countless musicians in New York, Boston, and Philadelphia, she set up shop on Forbes Avenue.

"I always had dreams of the stage, but for now, the doorway of Murphy's has to suffice," Betty says.

"I thought, 'I have a marketable talent. I'm going to see what I can do with it.' I just went out there and started playing, never expecting it to mushroom the way it has.

"Everybody in the city knows me. I guess getting punched in the schnozz had something to do with that," she says, referring to a publicized mugging two years ago. "I of course fought back," she adds.

Every business day, unless it's below freezing, she heads downtown to put in around three hours. She considers it a job, and doesn't believe she's "begging." I feel I'm giving a service because I'm a good musician. I'm not just playing sour notes out there," she says.

She reads music with the help of strong glasses, but says it puts her about a measure behind if she's playing with other musicians. Most of the time she memorizes pieces or plays by ear.

Sometimes she'll play a tin whistle a friend brought her from Ireland. Her eclectic repertoire goes beyond classical music to Mario Lanza and John Denver. "I won't get into the heavy metal, hard rock stuff. I just don't like it. Everybody tells me, 'Why don't you play rock flute? Why don't you play blues?' That's just not me."

Betty loves opera—especially Puccini, and has done flute arrangements of medleys from *La Traviata* and *Carmen*. She got a standing ovation at the Dravosburg Lioness Club for her rendition of *La Boheme*. She played the flute while lying on the floor for the aria from Mimi's death scene.

She also does a comedy sketch during indoor stage performances—"The Occupational Hazards of Being Blind or Partially Sighted," which she created to educate people about the function of guide dogs. She's amused by riding PAT buses and overhearing whispered comments about her dog being allowed to ride on public transportation. "I'm not *deaf*," she'll tell the crowd. "What do they expect—an alligator?"

Behind the street performer is an energetic, intelligent, and witty woman with a variety of interests. She and a friend, singer Maureen Wilkins, worked to establish a chapter of the Juvenile Diabetes Foundation here five years ago. She writes for the Northside Chronicle. Her cozy North Side apartment is filled with a massive doll collection, including some early Barbies.

The flutist she most admires is James Galway. "He always does the unusual. Someone walked by one cold, blustery, winter day and said to me, 'Ah, the James Galway of Pittsburgh.'

"I looked at him and said, 'Thank you, sir, that's really nice, but Jimmy has a nice, warm stage.' "

▲

# Hollywood on the Mon

By Abby Mendelson

The sky is leaden over Braddock Avenue. Stores are boarded up, and desolation hangs in the air. A disaster of a town, Braddock has lost most of its people, and its hope.

Unlike some, filmmaker Tony Buba has no idyllic vision of the past, when the Avenue bustled and pockets jingled, when there was pollution, shoddy housing, and white flight. "This area was never in great shape," he says. "When you fall into nostalgia, you tend to forget all that.

"There was a deep feeling on the part of the people who lived in Braddock," he adds. "They loved the town. Then they all moved out."

Buba didn't. Short and stocky and 46, he lives and works in a white frame house decorated largely in film posters and religious artifacts, a house that shares a common wall with his parents. Boss, a dog roughly the size of a pickup truck, thumps at the doors and windows. Buba genially ignores him.

Never a film buff as a child, Buba followed high school working in a plumbing supply house and on an electric range assembly line, where, one day while daydreaming, he riveted his finger to a circuit board.

Buba later drifted into college, finally wandering into film, and became the recipient of numerous grants. He's done weddings and industrial assignments to keep going, taught at the Pittsburgh Filmmakers, worked with horror master George Romero, and most of all, has remained loyal to his vision, his town.

Indeed, in his films there's the inescapable feeling that Buba *can't* leave, that his fate is to witness the destruction of the river towns. "There was a lot of poverty," he says in *Lightning Over Braddock*, "a lot of anger, and a lot of daydreaming."

He's made fifteen films about the demise of Braddock, its luncheonettes and bars, used car lots and jewelry stores, and aging, fading people, shooting his subjects as he finds them, then editing on the second floor of his house. His most ambitious and most distributed film is *Lightning Over Braddock*. Subtitled *A Rustbowl Fantasy*, the subject is as much about Buba as anything, his own low-key hopes and marginal career. A kaleidoscope of a movie, *Lightning Over Braddock* is a loopy, self-deprecating work which mixes equal parts of social consciousness, surrealism, and self-promotion.

There's footage of near-deserted Braddock Avenue, worker rallies, Jesse Jackson, a techno-pop dance in a steel mill, and other send-ups. In an ironic, off-beat way, the film is driven by Buba's stormy relationship with Sweet Sal Caru, a lizardy street hustler who growls and curses and chain smokes from start to finish. Sal, funny but immensely unlikable, appears as himself, and as Gandhi, Rambo, the Godfather. Sal emerges as a complex symbol of anger and paranoia, of betrayal, of crazy dreams and washed-out hopes. Ultimately, Sal stands for Buba's own disillusionment and ambivalence, for a man who spends his life making documentaries that never sell.

Or sell enough.

The award-winning *Lightning Over Braddock,* his most successful film, took five years to make, off and on, and cost $50,000. It was picked up by a New York distributor; went to film festivals in Toronto, San Francisco, England, Germany, and Portugal (all accompanied by the star, producer, director himself); it played nationwide at out-of-the-mainstream theaters, and was reviewed favorably by *The Washington Post, The New Yorker*, and *The New York Times*. At one point, Orion and Turner considered distributing it. Buba, forever realistic, knew neither would. They didn't. And he still needs $10,000 to break even.

For all that, Buba says and shrugs, "I'm doing better than I ever thought I would."

He's had some success, notably Guggenheim and Rockefeller grants. The latter, in fact, came just at the right time. Free-lance industrial work had dried up, and his wedding videos, all for relatives, had been disasters. "By the time I'd finished one couple," he laughs, "they were divorced. So for the last three years I've been pretty lucky. I haven't had to work."

Of course the game is getting funding, and it's a constant struggle. "It doesn't depend on your track record," Buba says. "You're hot for only so long in getting grants. You have to do something new all the time, or they're off to somebody else."

The Rockefeller has enabled Buba to move in a new direction, to put down his camera and pick up a pencil (or, more accurately, a word processor), and compose a full-length script about attitude changes in Braddock, the '60s brought into the '90s. "I don't want to do a coming-of-age film," he says, "to fall into the *Wonder Years* trap. That's been done so many times. What good is another one? I want to challenge myself until I fail."

Buba wants to focus on issues like racism, unemployment, Vietnam. Of course he fears that when the Rockefeller runs out there won't be anything to replace it. "The chances of getting funded are slim," Buba admits, "because the commercial potential is nil."

He knows all about it—his film about Braddockers who've gone to war was shelved because he couldn't find money for it.

Well, how about selling out? he's asked.

"Chase scenes?" he snorts. "I never think that way. Besides, I'm having a good time doing what I'm doing. I like those conflicts within myself—the mood swings, the three-day depressions. I've never been overly ambitious. I've never had a burning ambition to be a filmmaker, to be a success. I kind of fell into this."

▲

# A Singularly Plural Attraction

By Adrian McCoy

For an entertainer extraordinaire, Frankie Capri is a humble guy. He believes whatever musical talent he has is heaven-sent. "God made the pizza," Frankie says. "I just deliver it."

The pizza—and the toppings—do appear to be from another dimension. You have to see Frankie's magical kingdom a couple times before you can watch with your mouth closed. On Fridays he holds court at the Liberty Belle Lounge on the South Side.

Frankie is pegged as a one-man band, which is a pale, generic label for what he does. He's not exactly *alone* out there on stage. He's backed by a tiny orchestra—a bizarre furry ensemble of electric-powered monkeys that bang noiselessly on drums and cymbals and blow silent horns. Their attitude is workmanlike and competent, even if they don't make a sound. The stage is a riotous carnival of clowns and stuffed animals, framed by a string of anemic twinkling Christmas lights.

In the middle of it all, there's Frankie at the musical command center—two keyboard synthesizers, kazoo, and occasional accordion. The sounds Frankie squeezes out of these things are diverse and sometimes not quite of this world.

In the course of an evening, he'll take his audience from Vegas to vaudeville. He plays polkas and Irish tunes, and sings everybody's hits: Dean Martin, Jimmy Durante, Frank Sinatra, Tiny Tim, and Elvis. Although Frankie's a walking anthology of pop music, his own favorite performer is Mario Lanza.

He says playing one kind of music is boring. He wants the act to be a kind of live *Ed Sullivan Show,* with something for everybody—music, a little magic, and a few "clean" jokes.

Only Frankie *is* all the acts. "I make my own guests," he explains.

If you hear of an Elvis sighting on the South Side, there's a scientific explanation. It's just Frankie kicking into overdrive. As the night grows old, the crowd gets younger, a strobe starts flashing and Frankie's lounge act personalities take a back seat. How he can sing like the King and make a couple of Sears keyboards sound like a raw rockabilly band is part of the mystery.

"You try to simulate these entertainers in the people's minds. You ain't getting Elvis Presley, but you're getting something similar," Frankie says.

The monkeys—"my Calabrese monkeys," he calls them—were picked up from an antique dealer.

"God wanted me to have those monkeys," he says. One fateful day, he saw one of them playing cymbals in a store window. He went in to close the deal and found out the monkey was part of a set.

Frankie had a band.

Then there's Pasquale, the clown that flips his wig, and Luigi, a mannequin with a moving mouth. Luigi and Pasquale were previously employed as window dressings in a New York City department store.

"These people keep me company," Frankie says. "They're nice to work with."

He also has a toy dog and a stuffed Miss Piggy. Two Italian flags stand in tribute to his mother and father. Every week, he adds something new. He packs it all in his car, loading and unloading it several times a week.

"I get calls from guys who say, 'I got a little place. Can you come without the stuff?' I could do that, but I don't want to."

It takes about two hours to reconstruct the set. "I'm willing to spend the time. I love this. It's like a toy train with me," Frankie says. He does his own maintenance—oiling and fixing the little monkeys' mechanized guts. "In this business, you not only have to be a musician, you have to have a little imagination. You have to be a maintenance man, an electrician, a plumber," he says.

It keeps him unique. "I know there's nobody who's going to copy this thing." He's right there: Only Salvador Dali and Walt Disney working as a team could have hoped to duplicate it.

There's a logical history behind Frankie's colorful visions. He was born in McKeesport and raised in Italy. Now he's back in McKeesport. He learned to play accordion as a child, and performed in a combo with his brothers during the '50s.

Frankie didn't always make his living by being a musician. He used to be a barber. It was an okay living until the late '60s, when guys stopped getting haircuts every two weeks. Business dropped off.

"It used to be, people wanted a haircut, they went to Tony's barbershop. Tony's barbershop charges two dollars for a haircut. They don't want that. They want you to change your name to Antonino and charge them twenty dollars."

As if that weren't enough, DJs and canned music wiped out a lot of business for live bands, so Frankie went solo about eight years ago, and added the characters three years ago.

Frankie is as surprised as anyone to see his unusual act go over big with the babushka and brie crowds. A little fame in the corner pocket of western Pennsylvania is just fine with him. The big time eludes most dreamers. With Frankie, it's the other way around. Fifty thousand people at an arena, or fifty at the Liberty Belle—it's all the same to him. Mostly, he plays the local Moose and Elks circuit. He also does weddings.

But his fame is spreading. He was invited to Cleveland to play at Babylon A Go Go. "I got a good reception—beautiful," he says. "They gave me the red carpet treatment. They had lights flashing outside. I said, 'Man, who's appearing here tonight?' "

▲

# A Different Drummer

# By Roy McHugh

Success spoil Bob Drum? There was never the remotest chance. When Drum's face (which told the story of his life; it said that he'd been around the block) became familiar all of a sudden to television viewers, somebody asked his wife, Marian Jane, how it felt to be married to a celebrity.

"No different," she answered. "My husband thinks he was always a celebrity."

In 1984, Drum had been the ultimate late bloomer—an overnight success at the age of 66 as a sportscaster assigned to the professional golf tour.

Ordinarily when there's a golf tournament, the camera will focus on Curtis Strange, or someone, lining up a putt while the hushed, reverent tones of a disembodied voice let the audience know that Curtis Strange, or someone, is lining up a putt. The disembodied voice never was Drum's. What Drum did was interview people, usually in a flip, facetious way, and deliver short monologues, in which, as one critic wrote, he "stepped on toes and tweaked noses." Newspaper and magazine writers took to calling him "the

Andy Rooney of Golf," but Drum was Drum, no one else, and blissfully unaware of being newly discovered.

It was true that, for forty years, going back to his days at *The Pittsburgh Press*, Drum had cut a swath here and there. Now he was finding out that you could actually get paid for cutting a swath, and paid well. Success opened his eyes to the connection between money and work.

In his previous careers (as sportswriter, publicist, golf coach, salesman, and restaurant owner, not to mention round peg in square hole; very round peg at times—his weight goes up and down, and when it's up it is close to three hundred pounds), the notion had simply never occurred to Drum that money was work's reward. He appeared to regard a job, when he had one, as an unreasonable infringement on his personal liberty. Mind you, Frank Chirkinian, an executive producer with the Columbia Broadcasting System, was aware of all this when he offered Drum employment writing scripts. "It was not something I thought about, it was just something I did," Chirkinian apologized.

Drum, finding himself on the payroll, turned out a script or two for Pat Summerall and Ken Venturi, the CBS golf announcers, and then a lower-echelon producer, a man

named David Winner, came up with a prop-
osition that made thought unavoidable for
Chirkinian.

He suggested putting Drum on the tube.

Chirkinian thought about that for at least
thirty seconds and finally told Winner, "It's
either the best idea you've ever had or the
worst. Give it a try."

Drum had no experience, no training. His
face, compared rather extravagantly by CBS
announcer Ben Wright to a relief map of the
Andes, was beyond any help that the makeup
artists could provide. As for his voice, even
Winner described it as "gravelly." To others,
it sounded like gravel falling out of a dump
truck.

Winner wasn't bothered by any of that. In
clubhouse barrooms from Myrtle Beach to
Pebble Beach (Drum's natural habitat), Winner had heard him talk, and had noticed that
he could make people listen. There was no
easy way to ignore Drum. Just his size—in
addition to weighing whatever he weighs, he
is six feet three—guaranteed him an audience, and though it might not invariably be
an admiring audience, nobody ever tuned
out.

At St. Andrews one time—that's "historic"
St. Andrews, where the British Open is
played about every other year—Drum was in

the bar being the center of attention, as usual, while, off by themselves, a small, silent Scot and his wife sat and stared. Drum's stories were getting laughs from the golf writers clustered around him. Half an hour went by; the hilarity increased. At last, feeling expansive, Drum announced to the group: "I'm welcome any place in the world."

Whereupon the Scot who had just looked and listened spoke up. He said:

"Once."

But Winner—and plenty of others—could listen to Drum night after night. "And I just kind of wondered," Winner recalls, "if he could translate that—that sitting around and talking—into a performance."

At the 1984 Western Open, Winner squeezed Drum into a CBS blazer, said, "We're going to put you on television," and guided him through a feature—a feature spoofing the notion that professional golfers are clones of one another: tall, blond, picture- perfect Caucasians who look alike, dress alike, talk alike, act alike, and hit the ball the same way. On camera, Drum seemed to be endorsing the stereotype, but meanwhile there were seques to such tournament golfers of note as Chi Chi Rodriguez (Hispanic), Jim Thorpe (black), and Craig Stadler (Caucasian but far from picture-perfect).

The reviews were beyond expectations. As Winner said afterward, "Everybody liked it. The Drummer's personality came through. He filled the screen with that marvelous leonine head. And the voice—the gravelly voice—was wonderful. For an on-the-air personality, the component parts of the Drummer"—Winner had fabricated a nickname for his prodigy—"are the last thing you'd want, but even that worked in his favor."

Component parts and all, Drum became a fixture on the CBS telecasts. Under Winner's close tutelage, the style he developed was acerbic but not venomous. Example:

Winner might say to Drum, as he did on one occasion, "We've got to do a piece on Bob Tway. He's been playing so well."

Drum: "But I hate Bob Tway."

Winner: "He's the next Arnold Palmer." (Winner couldn't possibly have believed that.)

Drum: "But I hate Bob Tway."

Winner: "Well, that's the piece. That's what we're going to do, a profile of Bob Tway. We'll have you up there saying you hate Bob Tway, and then you'll explain why."

So, conversing with a straight man, Drum explained on the air why he hated Bob Tway: he envied the guy for his polish, his good looks, and his golf game. The straight man's line was, "You can't hate Bob Tway, he's the next Arnold Palmer," and Drum, in his best clubhouse barroom manner, came back with, "I hate Arnold Palmer too."

Drum was always able to take liberties with Palmer. They had known one another since the 1950s, when Drum covered golf for *The Press*. Palmer's future pre-eminence was so obvious so quickly to Drum that his colleagues on the golf beat, notably Dan Jenkins, accused him of inventing the man.

The fact was that Drum had invented a fairly large assortment of quotes he attributed to Palmer. "Do you know how many Arnold Palmer stories I wrote?" Drum asks rhetorically. "Five thousand, quoting him in every one, and half the time he was never around to talk to."

Palmer now believes that he said all those things, according to Drum.

In 1960, Drum saw to it personally, as he later told the story, that Palmer won the U.S. Open. The Open that year was played at the Cherry Hills course in Denver. Eight strokes behind after fifty-four holes, Palmer speculated to Drum that with a sixty-five on the last round he could still catch the leader. "What do you think?" Palmer asked. What Drum said he thought was that, for Palmer, a sixty-five wouldn't help. He had played himself out of the tournament. Infuriated, Palmer strode to the tee and drove the first green, three hundred forty-six yards away.

He birdied six of the first seven holes, shot the sixty-five he was talking about, and finished ahead of the field.

"I motivated him," Drum said.

As a sportswriter for *The Press,* Drum himself needed frequent motivation. There was nothing he disdained like the everyday routine of blue-collar journalism—the hum-Drum work, you might say. If a conflict existed between a hockey game and his plans for a Saturday night, he would swiftly compose, ahead of time, three different stories—one in the event of a home-team victory, one in the event of a home-team defeat, and one in the event of a tie. Blank spaces would be left for the final score and for the names of the players to be credited with goals and assists. Entrusting all three versions to the telegraph operator, with instructions to select the right one and fill in the missing details at the end of the game, Drum then would be off on pursuits of his own.

At other times he employed, with his own funds, a ghost writer, most often the hockey reporter for the *Post-Gazette.* One of the more unconventional hockey stories to appear under his byline was the work of a *Press* city-side reporter who had spent the afternoon over aperitifs and did not know a puck from a hole in the ice, having never before witnessed a game.

As a second-string football reporter, Drum

made it a rule to be physically present at the games he covered and would stay to the end if there wasn't any reason not to. Once with Penn State far ahead of Boston University at the half, Drum wrote his story, left a blank space for the final score, handed the sheets to the telegraph operator, and departed. Boston U.'s gallant second-half comeback, all but turning the tide, thus went undetailed in the Sunday morning *Press*.

At Carnegie Tech games, Drum diverted himself by bringing along a television set, plugging it into the only outlet—inconveniently located on the exterior wall of the press box—and from the top row of the stands, with his back to the action on the field, watching more glamorous teams, such as Pitt or Notre Dame.

His office hours, if any, were from 11 A.M. to 11:30 A.M. Executive sports editor Al Tederstrom was working on a piece of copy one day when a stranger approached his desk and asked, "Is Bob Drum here?"

"No," said Tederstrom, without raising his head.

"Do you know when he'll be in?"

"No."

"Do you know where he is?"

"No."

"Well, I'm his father," said the visitor, irritated. "I live in New York. I'm just passing

through, and I'd like to find him. I don't get
to see Bob very often."

Looking up for the first time, Tederstrom
said, "Neither do we."

Indeed, Drum was not one to sit all day at
a typewriter, agonizing over his prose. To say
that he could write fast understates it. A. J.
Liebling used to boast that he could write
faster than anyone who could write better,
and write better than anyone who could
write faster. Drum could write faster than
anyone who could write better. The second
half of the analogy doesn't apply, because no
one who ever lived could write faster than
Drum.

Arnold Palmer's administrative assistant,
Doc Giffin, worked at *The Press* with Drum,
and there were nights when they both covered basketball games. "Back in the office,"
Giffin once said, "we'd start to write our stories at the same time, and before I could get
past my byline, Drum would be finished and
gone."

He never groped for a word, never crossed
one out, never revised. Nothing distracted
him. Sometimes, late at night, he would go
from a sporting event to Dante's, a hangout
in Brentwood, write his story in longhand on
a cocktail napkin or the back of a menu, and
send it to the office by taxicab—collect.

Drum's other great asset as a newspaperman was the ability to out-think his mistakes. Once when the first edition came off the press, he happened, as luck would have it, to be in the office, and was brought up short by the headline on something he had written. Accurately reflecting the information in Drum's story, the headline informed his readers that a golf event called the Diebold Cup Matches would be played that very day at one of the country clubs. Drum now realized that the matches would not be played until the following week. In such emergencies he was never found wanting. He busied himself for a minute or two making changes, and the headline in the second edition read: "Diebold Cup Matches Postponed."

Drum was temperamentally unsuited for covering stories of less than major significance. The bigger the challenge the better he performed. On the final day of the 1960 U.S. Open, the Professional Golfers' Association offered a prize for the best opening paragraph. Drum's lead, a snappy pugilistic metaphor, won. Meanwhile, back at *The Press*, an assistant managing editor was having it rewritten in the who-what-where-when formula deemed appropriate for page-one news, which the U.S. Open, because of Palmer's victory, had become.

For Drum and his editors to be on different pages, so to speak, was nothing new. By

accident, almost, he had landed a job with
*The Press* in 1945. The paper was short-
handed as a result of the war, and Drum's
Army combat service had earned him an
early discharge. Equally pertinent, his father
had a speaking acquaintance with someone in
top management—either a Scripps or a
Howard, Drum has forgotten which. For reasons which now seem obscure to him, but
may have stemmed from the fact that he had
been an all-around athlete, first at Lynn-
brook High School on Long Island and then,
not very gloriously, at the University of Ala-
bama, he aspired to a career as a sportswriter, and *The Press* started him out at the
standard munificent beginner's salary, $32.50
a week.

Drum was worth every cent of it, but he
discovered in short order that sportswriting
as a profession was overrated. As his relations
with his editors cooled, so did Drum's enthu-
siasm. He was interested only in covering the
important golf tournaments, and when trans-
atlantic plane trips were involved, the paper
kept him at home. Drum attended the 1963
British Open as a guest of the PGA (the annual match between the British and American golf writers required his participation, it
seems) but with orders not to file any copy.
So for three days, relying on the wire services, the paper saved money. It worked out

just fine until Arnold Palmer, regarded by *The Press* as a home-town boy, moved into second place with eighteen holes to play. Adjusting to the change in the outlook, Drum's managing editor sent him a cable: "Need story for tomorrow on Palmer." Drum cabled back: "I hope you get one."

His subsequent departure from the newspaper business was not altogether unpredictable.

To support his wife and their five growing children, Drum did publicity for the promoters of various golf tournaments and continued to write the books and magazine articles with which for years he had augmented his pay. He could polish off a book in two or three days, but gathering the material took time. Often the research was arduous, as when Drum wrote a biography of Steeler quarterback Bobby Layne that required him to spend evenings at the Point View Hotel, where some of the best jazz in town could be heard and where the evenings turned into dawns with Layne still calling for encores from the band.

Barely forty years old and at the height of his prowess as a bon vivant, Drum had tremendous absorptive capacity, but keeping up with Layne, a much smaller man with what eventually proved to be a much less durable liver, was impossible. One night when Layne refused to quit, Drum ignominiously left by

the back door. It was 4 A.M. on a Sunday in
December. Drum went home and fell into
bed. He slept until the afternoon and was
late for the kickoff at Pitt Stadium, where the
Steelers were playing the Chicago Cardinals.
Just as Drum arrived, Layne threw a touchdown pass, his third of the game. On an
ice-covered field, Layne also ran for a
touchdown that day and broke the Steeler
record for passing yardage.

Layne spent the winters in Lubbock,
Texas, and Drum flew down there in February for one last interview. Reasoning that
Texas was in the South, he wore a seersucker
suit, sneakers (Drum may have pioneered the
fashion) and no topcoat. At the Lubbock airport, borrowing fifty dollars from Layne, he
tipped the jazz band Layne had hired to ser-
enade him. The next thing Drum knew, he
was flying with Layne to Aspen, Colorado.
Layne's old Detroit Lion teammate, Doak
Walker, had gone there for the skiing, and
Layne wanted Walker in the book. In the Aspen snowdrifts, Drum lost one of his sneakers, and in the sauna room at the ski lodge
he lost the notes he had taken. Not in the
least incommoded, he flew back to Pittsburgh half shod, and wrote the book out of
his head.

All of his books were "worst sellers,"
Drum admits. Even his Arnold Palmer book,
*Hit It Hard*, was a worst seller. *Hit It Hard*

was an instructional book, which Drum says he wrote by himself, with no help from Palmer. "I cribbed it from other golf books— all of them say the same thing. When the book came out, Palmer didn't read it," Drum says. Aware that his own game could stand improvement, Drum went to Palmer for a lesson. He says that Palmer advised him to read *Hit It Hard* calling it "his" (Palmer's) book and claiming, "Everything you need to know is in there."

Willy-nilly, Drum had acquired a true understanding of technique and tactics. At the British Open one year, spotting a tiny defect in Palmer's putting stroke, he mentioned it to Winnie Palmer, Arnold's wife, who mentioned it to her husband, who corrected the flaw. On another occasion, Drum soundly berated Jack Nicklaus for his undue conservatism on the tee. "You're the longest and straightest driver in the history of golf, and you're fooling around with three-woods and one-irons. It's a disgrace!" Drum fulminated. Obediently, Nicklaus changed his ways. In Drum's mail the next month there came an autographed picture of Nicklaus leaning happily on the club he had just used to win the PGA tournament—his driver.

Cashing in on his reputation as a giver of valuable counsel, Drum became the golf coach at Virginia Military Institute. In the bargain, he served as sports information director. But the academic world could not contain him for long, and by the late 1960s he was selling capacitors in upstate New York. Think nothing of it if you don't happen to know what capacitors are. Neither does Drum. "I knew we had big ones and little ones, but no mediums," he vaguely recalls. Prospering from the sale of the big ones and little ones, he invested in a restaurant on Hilton Head Island and managed it for a time. Meanwhile, at all of the major golf tournaments, he was doing freelance radio work, interviewing the players as they finished their rounds. Chirkinian, who liked to talk about hiring Drum on a whim, had a perfectly logical reason as well: Drum's "knowledge of the game and its lore."

Television, the medium of direct communication, was made to order for Drum, who is nothing if not direct. And television magnified a dimension of Drum that was lost on the printed page. Call it stage presence. Or, sure—why not?—star quality. "He's a very popular guy," said another very popular guy, Arnold Palmer, when Drum was riding high. "It's amazing the success he has seen in— what shall I call them?—his twilight years," Palmer went on, bemused.

In 1989, a victim of the cost-cutting orgy at CBS, Drum was off the air. In 1990, he was back again, appearing every week on "The Golf Show," a syndicated program carried by WWOR.

So, yes—there is life after CBS, even at seventysomething.

Reviewing his accomplishments, Drum once congratulated himself on having triumphed over the three worst afflictions there are—cancer, poverty, and matrimony. Exactly right. Three decades ago, he licked the Big C; in the periodically fell clutch of circumstance, he has kept some insistent wolves from the door; and though their golden anniversary relentlessly approaches, he remains on good terms with Marian Jane. Be assured that if poverty comes back for a rematch, Drum will have weapons to fight it.

Gamely, he perseveres, the twilight years receding before him.

▲

# A Craftsman's Touch

By Abby Mendelson

It's a lazy Sunday morning, and Bill Strickland, with coffee and cigarettes, ambles into the Manchester Craftsmen's Guild studio on the North Side.

Tall and black and lanky, Strickland strips down to his T-shirt and khakis, rips off a big hunk of clay with his long fingers and rolls it into a cone. He slaps the clay down on a still potter's wheel, then turns it on. Wetting his fingers in a pink plastic bucket, Strickland runs them up and down the cone. He presses his thumb in the center, then draws the clay out and into a tall column, the dark, wet mass squirting around his fingers.

The walls swirl up high—a vase—then low and wide—a flat dish. Satisfied with the shape, Strickland uses a small sponge to refine the walls, then a piece of hard rubber to smooth the floor. A swift, sure knife cut takes off excess height, and a wire with two handles slices the bottom so the clay will dry evenly.

It's all so easy.

Articulate and easy going,, Strickland is the 42-year-old son of a building tradesman.

After working clay in high school, he formed the Manchester Craftsmen's Guild while still at Pitt, hoping to use clay to get to street kids. If the mixture didn't entirely work, Strickland learned valuable lessons about organizational skills, funding, creating a board, writing grants. Most important, he says, "I began to figure out ways to deal with these kids."

As a bright, eager Pitt grad, Strickland could have been anything he wanted to be. He wanted to fly, so became a commercial airline pilot, flying on weekends, working in Manchester during the week. In 1972 he was named executive director of grant-supported Bidwell Training Center, a job training facility now in a multi-million-dollar building on Metropolitan Street. Bidwell, which also houses the Craftsmen's Guild, is an impressive structure, with large tapestries, paintings and photos on the walls, sculpture in the corridors, a concert hall—plus computer, medical technology, and culinary arts classrooms and laboratories.

The plan, he says, was influenced by the style of Frank Lloyd Wright, for whom art was an integral part of daily living, even—or especially—down to lighting and windows. "If you use art every day," Strickland says, "it becomes a pattern, a way of perceiving the world."

Under Strickland's leadership, job placement for his trainees runs about ninety percent, which is one reason many Pittsburgh corporations and foundations fund Bidwell. Strickland shrugs. Success hasn't changed him. Or his art.

As an artist, Strickland does not want—or need—the feedback or recognition that so many thrive on. Although widely known as a potter, he never shows or sells his work, instead preferring simply to give it to friends. "I do it as a personal thing," he says.

Making the plate and letting it dry for a day or two are only the first stages. Next there's the bisque kiln, one thousand six hundred degrees of wall-to-wall heat, to further harden the clay. Then the glaze, these days four or five basic colors Strickland's been inspired to work with. While he may have a rough idea of color when he dabs it on, due to the vagaries of clay and pigment and firing, the end result is always a surprise. "That's why it's an art," he says, "and not a product." Finally, the last firing, two thousand four hundred degrees, until the clay becomes stone.

He likes clay, he says, because of its "plasticity. It's an immediately responsive material, one that has an ability to create a form instantaneously." For inspiration, he says, all he has to do is look out the window at "the whole picture of the Ohio Valley, its configurations and its changes. A gray day is a gray day—with countless variances. Because light moves and shifts, and changes what you see, and what you feel about what you see. It changes the way I feel about my pottery."

That sort of fluid vision came early, he says, "when I was three years old, sitting on my mother's lap, seeing cloud patterns—and innumerable life possibilities. Now what I'm about is trying to create a series of daily possibilities for people—jazz, computers, culinary arts, clay. It's all the same thing, just different tools."

He does it in a place he built himself, living and working within walking distance of where he was brought up. When Strickland grew up, Manchester was a multi-ethnic neighborhood, and he reveled in the mix of different cultures. "That was my habitat, and I wanted to reproduce my life environment as a kid. It's a straight-line shot from then to now. That's why I insisted Bidwell be a multi-racial school. And it had to be here. I wanted to preserve that part of Pittsburgh that has to do with relationships.

"Besides," he adds, "when you articulate a philosophy of helping people, you have to do it completely. You have to mean it. I'm not that fascinated with the big conquest. I'm a textbook Pittsburgher—I don't like to be in unfamiliar places. I really have a small-town way of looking at things. And Pittsburgh *is* a small town."

Strickland holds up a finished serving plate, deep blue with a rusty red area in the middle and a harder red around the edge. In the subtle mix of colors he sees the summer sky, at dusk, after a storm has passed, when the colors are fading and mottled. "When I was younger," he says, "I thought I would change this and change that. But when you see life patterns emerging, you see that getting through with some dignity and some sanity is a full-time gig. I've been happy with these. They are canvases, and the glaze becomes paint."

# Serial Killing for Profit

By Paul Maryniak

**E**verybody understood why the cleaning lady had screamed.

This was not a matter of missing linens, stolen towels, or furniture battered by drunken rock musicians.

No, thought the detectives, lab technicians, and morgue attendants, few people could have avoided doing what the maid did when she opened the door to Room 239 in the obscure motel on the second story of the main terminal at Greater Pittsburgh International Airport in the early afternoon of May 18, 1979.

Accustomed as they had become to grisly crime scenes, the small army of Allegheny County homicide investigators themselves couldn't help but flinch when they saw their next case.

Sprawled on the floor near the bed was a mangled woman who gave new meaning to the eleven A.M. checkout policy. Someone with a gun and a knife had made sure she checked out permanently—very sure, very permanently.

The autopsy would detail more than enough carnage to terrify even the most jaded charlady. The pathologist listed thirty-two stab wounds in the chest, at least twelve in the neck, another nine in the back. A surgical-style slash ran clear across her throat from ear to ear. In all, there were sixty-eight incisions and punctures ranging in length from one to five inches. One .22-caliber bullet wound was found over her left eye, another in her upper left forehead, a third in the back of her skull. From distinctive markings on the bullets, ballistics experts concluded the gun likely had been equipped with a silencer.

Someone really enjoyed this mutilation, or got really furious, or both.

The homicide team from the county and its counterpart in the Pittsburgh Police Department had seen similarly frenzied slaughter over the previous five years. Along with an equally brutal slaying farther east in adjoining Westmoreland County, the crimes fit a loose pattern that no lawman could decipher.

In four cases, the victims went to their graves in a hail of gunfire, a flurry of slashes and thrusts from a knife, or both. One victim had been blown apart, literally. All had things in common with the woman on the floor in the motel: each had died in the second half of the month, a miscellaneous tidbit that initially was considered a possibly important feature, but ultimately never became relevant evidence. Each knew the others. Also, all had the same connection, however tenuous, to a particular kind of business in the Golden Triangle.

Although veiled, the business was the practice of the world's oldest profession—prostitution. The sale of sexual pleasures was hidden beneath a thin veneer of a renewed national interest in physical fitness and athletics.

The corpses were linked to the city's massage parlors.

The newspapers and TV overflowed with up-to-the-minute details of a war for control of the sin dens.

But they were covering a wild goose chase.

Even though the airport motel guest was no $20-a-jerk masseuse, it was only natural that the reporters and some police speculated 26-year-old Deborah Gentile was the latest casualty in an underworld struggle to monopolize the city's erotic zone, Liberty Avenue.

She had friends there, and one awful enemy.

But a phone call that May 18 from an FBI agent to county homicide Detectives Robert Payne and Michael Lackovic opened a new trail to follow after they finished working around Gentile's fully-clad but ravaged torso. With that call, the detectives and a grand jury began to unravel a more intricate, a far more diabolical web of greed and gore. The trail led to a man eventually suspected in thirty killings, including all but one of the slayings originally dubbed "the rub parlor hits."

The FBI agent—they love to call cops with tips and stay behind their desks—told Payne and Lackovic that Debbie Gentile had a relationship that the "federales" had been studying in connection with income tax evasion and interstate transportation of stolen gold and jewelry.

Take a look, the G-man said, at a guy named Richard Henkel. The FBI, as always, was very good at pointing a finger and then sitting back to watch the local fuzz do the work.

*     *     *

In mid-1974, the spirit of peace and love from the previous decade still hung like a cloud of marijuana smoke over the heads of psychologists and staffers at the federal penitentiary in Marion, Illinois. How else could they explain their incredibly misguided—and misguiding—evaluation that year of inmate Richard Henkel?

Here was this thug from the Greenfield section of Pittsburgh who had been considered enough of a threat to society that he was stuck in Marion, the strictest of all federal penitentiaries and one reserved for only the most ruthless cons prosecuted by the United States government. It is home to so many bad asses that countless assaults by inmates on inmates, and inmates on guards, led to permanent lockdown—meaning the inhabitants were out of their cages only minutes a day for exercise. The grounds are encircled with miles of entangled wire made from razor blades, and yet there have been escapes, ingenious ones.

This was home to Richie Henkel back in 1973, before the lockdown but well into the era when Marion had the reputation as the place where the hardest of the hardcore were walled.

Marion staffers wanted to let Henkel go— not to a less oppressive prison, but out into the world.

He had been sent to Marion in late 1970, after a brief stay in a federal pen in Atlanta, to continue a twenty-year sentence for bank robbery. On the surface, his crimes didn't seem to merit the harsh confines of Marion.

Previous to Atlanta he had served only about a year in jail, despite more than a dozen arrests for credit card fraud, burglary, and counterfeiting.

Officials in Atlanta felt Henkel exerted a bad influence on the inmates around him. It was almost as if he put them under a spell. Smarter than the average con, Henkel seemed to have no trouble getting inmates to do his bidding through a deft combination of threats and entreaties, promises and compliments.

Yet, by 1973, the staff at Marion was looking at him in an entirely different light. Henkel had begun to focus his seductive powers on the zookeepers rather than on the animals.

Only three years had passed since Henkel was charged with being one of two bare-faced gunmen who walked into the Duquesne Heights branch of Keystone Bank on July 24, 1969, and got away with $80,000 in cash. Henkel and his accomplice, a professional stickup artist from Squirrel Hill named Lawrence Windsor, were positively identified by witnesses in the bank and those along the getaway route. The two men dashed out of the bank, got into a car, and eventually abandoned the vehicle a few miles away.

During his trial, Henkel adopted a not-too-original line of defense. He said it was all a horrible mistake, that the cops got the wrong man. He presented alibi testimony from relatives who said he was with them watching the televised splashdown of the Apollo 11 moonwalkers.

The jury quickly realized he was sincerely interested in tales of outer space; Henkel produced a pitiful patsy to take the fall. Of course, when the stand-in said he and Windsor planned and executed the heist, it wasn't as if 25-year-old Peter Biagiarelli of Homestead had a lot to lose by saying these things under oath. He already was facing certain conviction on a murder charge carrying an automatic life sentence for killing a Viet Nam war veteran in a $6 holdup.

Biagiarelli had an answer for almost every question that the federal prosecutor put to him during Henkel's bank robbery trial. The fallguy carefully explained how he and Windsor had given Henkel the $20,000 found in Henkel's safe deposit box. And to explain the sudden desire to come clean with the crime, Biagiarelli informed the jury that Henkel said "if I didn't, he'd tell on me."

Biagiarelli was nearly an unshakeable witness under cross examination, but only nearly.

To shoot down the story, federal prosecutors had twelve people in the courtroom gallery stand up. Then Biagiarelli was asked to pick out anyone he remembered from the bank job. Biagiarelli was speechless. He couldn't pick out a single one—even though five of those standing were tellers who had been instructed at gunpoint to stuff cash into bags.

Of course, he could explain that, too. He said that on the day in question he was not wearing his eyeglasses. Thus, he said, his perfect disguise as Henkel's look-alike also had rendered him virtually blind; he just couldn't see anyone all that well.

A month after conviction on all counts, an unrepentant Henkel stood before U.S. District Judge Rabe F. Marsh at sentencing and continued asserting innocence. "The only thing wrong I did, possibly, was run," Henkel said. Unimpressed and unmoved, Marsh put him away for twenty years.

Windsor was never captured. In fact, he was seen for the last time about a week after the bank robbery. He battered his wife one night and stalked out of their home in a half-drunken rage, saying he was heading out "to play pool with the guys." Even the U.S. Attorney gave up on finding him, formally dismissing the outstanding charges against Windsor less than a year after Henkel went to jail. Ten more years passed before police finally figured out what probably happened to Windsor. Their theory had everything to do with his association with a man who didn't hesitate to bury partners in crime.

Biagiarelli was convicted of murdering the ex-serviceman and sentenced to life imprisonment at Western Penitentiary, where he too was recognized as a model prisoner—until he took advantage of a visit from his parents in December, 1976, to beat a guard, steal a gun, and escape to San Francisco. He was captured three months later.

Meanwhile, in the three years that followed his sentencing, Henkel was busy becoming a model prisoner, and, as far as federal parole officials were concerned, a living testament to the wonders of enlightened penitentiary management.

A grammar school dropout, he had earned a high school diploma behind bars. He maintained close to an A+ average in a two-year college program at Marion, then went on to an advanced course for a major in psychology. His choice of study was no mere accident: Henkel had a gift for understanding people, and, more importantly, for getting them to do things his way.

Henkel had no trouble, either, understanding the psychology of prison officials or getting them to do what he wanted. As a model prisoner, he joined the prison's Jaycee chapter, the Historical Society, the Euro-American Educational Association, and the

Outstanding Educators Association.

His psychology worked on the psychologists.

His teachers and school administrators showered him with praise. Their letters accompanied a petition filed in early 1974 in federal court by David O'Hanesian, a Pittsburgh lawyer who had represented him at trial.

Once a county prosecutor, O'Hanesian was a smoothie.

"Henkel has great remorse for the way his life has been wasted," O'Hanesian's petition declared, noting his client "attends church faithfully," and that his years in confinement "have had such a traumatic effect on him that it is my firm belief that Mr. Henkel will never again need the advice of a criminal lawyer."

Ultimately, he could have used a dozen—a dozen smoothies, in fact.

To further illustrate how Henkel had seen the light, O'Hanesian attached a glowing report from the administrator of the school. The report confidently declared that Richard Henkel was a "psychologically stable person interested in making a positive contribution to society."

With so many testimonials for the college grad, Marsh approved early parole.

The judge's decision soon was followed by

a murderous six-year fling. The one-time elementary school truant had gotten a real education while a guest of the government.

\* \* \*

By the time Debbie Gentile learned that Pittsburgh could be America's Most Unliveable City, the news media had lost all fascination with the so-called massage parlor war. The war had been reduced to a smoldering conflict by the late 1970s. Too much time passed between bodies, and there didn't seem to be much point to the struggle, because the rubdown joints themselves were in an economic struggle to stay open as much as steel mills. Besides, the victims weren't exactly pillars of the community and no newspaper demographic consultant would endorse a crusade for an end to the slaughter of pimps and hookers—especially at a time when newspapers were crusading for stronger lawn furniture to shore up sagging circulation in the suburbs.

In the mid 1970s, though, the body count was hot stuff.

Headlines trumpeted the war as politicians and police officials roared at the evils that resulted from unchecked vice. In a way, the slayings rekindled the dormant anti-pronography crusade that DA Robert W. Duggan had used so handily to win re-election at the beginning of the decade. In the early 1970s, he was raiding movie houses that were showing films of men and women, or women and women, making love. He even went to court to close shows that ten years later ran on late-night television. Duggan had two motives, besides making political hay, that were revealed after his death by self-inflicted gunshot: He was shaking down the theater owners for protection, and he personally abhorred sex between men and women, or between women and women, leaving but one other kind between humans.

The first Henkel victim materialized in 1975, but, ironically, no one suggested until much later that a massage parlor war—or any kind of underworld conflict, for that matter—was underway. There were more obvious, more compelling reasons why someone would have wanted to put sixteen rounds from a .22-caliber gun into the body, mainly the head, of a certain 40-year-old Richland Township horse trainer, thief, and dope peddler, Glenn Scott. When his body was discovered on November 23, 1975, Scott was only a few weeks away from a command performance before a special county grand jury investigating a crime that had captured far bolder headlines than the fabled massage parlor war.

At the time, he had emerged as a figure in the Manpower Scandal, named after a federally-funded program that the Allegheny County commissioners ostensibly ran to provide jobs for poor adults, and summer amusement for underprivileged youngsters. Like its corrupt predecessor, the short-lived Model Cities program of President Lyndon Johnson, the Manpower program in no time became a feeding trough for every two-bit hustler with a ward heeler in his pocket, and for every ward heeler with a two-bit hustler in his pocket, and for a select group in the middle.

Before the special grand jury began nailing a total of fifty-one defendants, more than $500,000 was stolen. Thousands of dollars worth of sports gear was purchased for poor kids and never reached the ghetto; questionable individuals—and imaginary ones—ended up on the public payrolls; suitcases of cash were carted to banks for deposits in private accounts.

Scott ran one of Manpower's summer youth programs. A year before his death, he had leased a ranch and spent thirty thousand dollars in tax grants to convert it into a camp. Despite his lengthy arrest record, Scott gained access to the public funds through the political connections of his friend, Pittsburgh Steeler running back

Franco Harris. Harris also received some of the cash handouts, as did his sister (a law student at Duquesne University), his girlfriend (an airline flight attendant), her brother, her mother, and several of Harris' Super Bowl teammates. Scott used his Manpower power to order riding gear, recreation equipment, and other expensive toys. Most of the merchants never were paid, and the money disappeared.

Scott wasn't connected to the massage parlor war at first—mainly because the Manpower Scandal connection was more logical.

As it turned out, both connections were fantasies, just hunches.

The first round in the heavily publicized rubdown parlor war was considered to have been fired two years later, when one racket overlord was shot three times by a fleet-footed assailant in a parking lot near the Edison Hotel, a landmark for the sleaze that overran the Golden Triangle after the sun went down.

Dead on February 24, 1977, was George E. Lee, once an ironworker who lived an unobtrusive suburban life in Baldwin Borough, but who in reality operated several massage parlors and call-girl rings Downtown. Lee faced his stiffest competition from a Mafia-backed felon, city fireman Nick DeLucia, and his top aide, a freakishly slovenly and overweight dyke, Dante "Tex" Gill. Although DeLucia and Gill benefitted from Lee's demise, police had nothing to link them to the hit—even though DeLucia was with Lee when he dropped.

After Lee was hit, police already had cause to wonder if war was being waged. About a week before Lee was gunned down, another competitor in the oil-and-jackoff trade, Mel Cummings, a former county construction inspector and bookie, narrowly missed three bullets fired from a passing car.

Lee's death became all the more baffling on December 12, 1977, when the manager of his Gemini Spa on Liberty Avenue was found dead. Anthony "Bobby" Pugh's body was discovered in a South Hills apartment that was leased to a woman who also had been in Lee's company at the time of his killing. Even though Pugh was only a deskman for the rub parlor, someone seemed to dislike him a great deal: he had been shot six times in the head with a .22.

Glenn Scott's slaying took on a whole new interpretation just two days before Christmas, 1977, when his widow, 21-year-old Joann "Sasha" Scott, learned the hard way that big things indeed come in small packages. Just as she was ready to call it a day as a masseuse at the Gemini Spa, a cab driver walked in and dropped off a package that he said had been given to him by a man wearing a Santa Claus mask and wig. The cab Driver took off, and Sasha uttered her last "Merry Christmas."

Sasha never had to worry about what to wear on New Year's Eve. She ripped the wrap from the package, opened the box, and triggered a horrendous explosion of shotgun shells that sent hundreds of metal washers and inch-and-a-half-long aluminum nails tearing through her body. Glass rained on Liberty Avenue, as did tiny bits of Sasha.

Unknown to city police detectives who began investigating the blast, the same kind of shrapnel had been used thousands of miles away two years earlier in a bombing with a slim Pittsburgh connection. That fragmentation bomb, mailed in a package postmarked from Pittsburgh's Oakland district, had killed a Vancouver, British Columbia, restaurateur. The U.S. Treasury's Bureau of Alcohol, Tobacco and Firearms eventually determined that out of twenty thousand explosive devices it had analyzed in a ten-year period, only the Gemini and Vancouver incidents involved that kind of shrapnel. Not until 1981 would police discover the reason for that remarkable coincidence.

The bombing at the Gemini and the other deaths set law enforcement brass on edge.

Mayor Richard Caliguiri sought an injunction to shut down the rub parlors, and city police officials demanded that a grand jury be empaneled to probe the vice district's bloody turn.

For a few months, some calm returned to the Golden Triangle.

And then on May 24, 1978, the New Kensington neighbors of Mafia underboss Kelly Mannarino complained about an odor coming from the trunk of a late model Oldsmobile that had been parked on the street for several days. New Kensington police opened the trunk and found the body of onetime masseuse Suzanne Dixon. She had been a Gemini attraction.

Where Dixon actually was killed was never learned. The New Kensington Police Department didn't seem to be in too great a hurry to find out, either. The car was not examined for a week after the corpse was discovered.

Some police officials in Westmoreland County told their counterparts across the boundary line in Pittsburgh that no one would find fingerprints anyway because the car had been sitting out in the rain. Other investigators cynically suggested that New Ken police were afraid to ask questions upsetting to the neighborhood's most prominent resident. Residents of New Kensington knew their don better than that—he could never be so dumb as to let the victim of a hit rot outside his own house.

When Gentile's corpse was discovered nineteen months later at the airport motel, Pittsburgh and Allegheny County cops became even more interested in the Dixon slaying.

Initially, their interest was sparked by the similarity between the two homicides. Like Gentile, Dixon was the victim of a killer who had gone amuck. She had been shot seven times in the head with a .22-caliber gun and had been stabbed seventeen times in the neck and chest; her throat had been laid open. The gun appeared to have been equipped with a silencer.

As they began unraveling Debbie Gentile's final days, detectives realized that she, Dixon, Pugh, and the Scotts shared one other connection that had nothing to do with massage parlors.

That connection was their friendship with a reformed ex-con, Henkel.

\* \* \*

To gain status as an early parole candidate, Henkel had impressed federal authorities with a newfound faith in God, and an unprecedented interest in academics. But when

he was released in early 1974 at the age of
36, the balding little man with hooded eyes
and a slightly high-pitched, scratchy voice
turned to people who probably had not seen
the inside of a church in decades, let alone
a book.

After renting a townhouse in Greentree
that he used when he wasn't staying in
Youngstown, Ohio, Henkel began hanging
around the notoriously shady Court Lounge
of gangster Joey DeMarco. Henkel also renewed contacts with a diverse array of individuals—all but one of them with prior
criminal records.

Before it came under the wrecking ball,
the Court Lounge was a popular watering
hole for judges, lawyers, pimps, strong-arm
men, hookers, and assorted nonclassifi-
able riff-raff. It was run—and believed by
his patrons to be owned—by the Brookline
mobster DeMarco, whose heroin dealing,
counterfeiting, and sundry other criminal activities made him a newsworthy host for the
Courthouse and City-County Building crowd
that turned to his nearby bar after a hard day
of public service.

Bending elbows with judges, barristers,
and local government bureaucrats and politicians at the Court Lounge were people like
Anthony "Ninny" Lagattuta, a torch; Anthony
Repepi, the aging guardian of Mafia gam-

bling interests in the Mon Valley; and dozens of runners for numbers boss Tony Grosso. And that was on a slow night.

Because the state Liquor Control Board ostensibly forbids certifiable scumballs like DeMarco from having liquor licenses, the Court Lounge on paper was owned by Suzanne Dixon. In 1979, about seventeen months after Dixon's body was found,by New Kensington police, DeMarco's bullet-riddled body was discovered on top of the spare tire in his luxury car in the short-term lot at Greater Pitt. A friend he was supposed to be meeting was missing and presumed dead. The DeMarco hit remains an open case, although police believe his killing was the handiwork of the same reformed ex-con who was proven responsible for the slayings of Gentile and the Scotts.

When he wasn't mingling with low-lifes at the Court Lounge, Henkel began rekindling his association with a group of Philadelphia hoods called the Hallmark Gang. Named for the exquisite taste in selecting only quality stuff from their victims, the gang members were indicted in 1979 in connection with the burglaries of wealthy families across the Eastern seaboard. In North Carolina alone, they were indicted for stealing more than half a million dollars of valuables from bank presidents, the widow of a former governor, and an heir to the Reynolds tobacco fortune. The

Hallmark Gang also was suspected in similar high-stakes burglaries in Fox Chapel and Sewickley. And the gang was linked to a rash of burglaries in posh eastern Pennsylvania suburbs, including one that ended in the deaths of a 77-year-old Bucks County couple in March, 1976.

The unusual aspect of that double homicide, which police believed was committed during a burglary, was that both victims apparently had been subdued with a taser gun, a weapon that momentarily paralyzes victims with a powerful electric shock. Then they died of single gunshot wounds to the head from different caliber revolvers. One of the revolvers eventually was recovered in a nearby creek and was discovered to have been taken from one of the North Carolina homes that had been ransacked by the Hallmark Gang.

Although the investigation into the Bucks County slayings hit a dead end, police managed to identify most of the members of the Hallmark Gang. They included Louis Kripplebauer and Bruce Agnew—two Philadelphians who frequented Henkel's Greentree apartment. A close friend of theirs was Jack Siggson, a convicted murderer who also had become part of Henkel's circle.

Henkel also wasn't the kind of person who forgot old friends. He stayed in close touch with Roy Travers, a Vancouver, British Columbia, con he met at the federal prison in Marion. Travers was an electronics genius who specialized in making eavesdropping and other devices from equipment available at Radio Shack.

Travers also had a fascination with—and a knack for making—explosive devices. That put him in good stead with Henkel's only friend who didn't have a rap sheet, a tall, blond and cold-eyed Edgewood police officer, Gary Small.

Small was an unusual law enforcement officer for any department, let alone that of the relatively tranquil bedroom borough of Edgewood. When he wasn't patrolling the streets of the tiny suburb just east of Pittsburgh, he was preparing for the day the Russians would invade: He participated in the weekend drills and other pastimes of a right-wing paramilitary group called the Minutemen.

Orphaned at an early age, Small was taken into the Henkel home by Richie's mother. When Henkel was released from prison in early 1974, the Edgewood cop returned the favor and gave him a temporary home at his place.

As police later found, Small and Henkel shared interests other than Hannah's home cooking. They were both fond of firearms—especially 9-millimeter and .22-caliber handguns. Witnesses later told police they had seen Small give Henkel several of those weapons, as well as silencers, which not even suburban cops are allowed to own under federal law.

With so many friends to help him re-adjust quickly to life outside the federal pen, Henkel lost little time picking up where he had left off when the FBI charged him with the bank holdup. His known specialties included burglaries, fencing hot jewelry in Florida and California, and drug dealing.

Henkel also began a new enterprise. He became a contract killer, sometimes swapping hits with a Youngstown hood named Joseph DeRose, who was considered a button man for organized crime in Cleveland.

As police eventually learned, Henkel often told his associates that he wanted to make a lot of money before his federal parole ended in 1990. But it wasn't too long before Henkel decided that he had told too much. So, in no time, his circle of friends began to shrink, literally.

For many of them, that circle became a noose—with Richard Henkel as its deadly knot.

\* \* \*

Despite the bloody mess in Room 239,

Debbie Gentile's killer was surprisingly neat. He never left so much as a smudged fingerprint, a strand of hair, or any clue that could be used by the detectives to track him down. Even though a half dozen USAir flight attendants had been partying in a room down the corridor, no one heard a sound. Detectives eventually discovered why. Once they learned through ballistics tests that a silencer had probably been used in the killing, they returned to the room with a .22 revolver, a silencer, and a decibel meter to measure sound. They test-fired the weapon and the meter barely registered.

Because of the hint they had received from the FBI, detectives were at Henkel's townhouse in Hampton within eight hours after Gentile's body was found. Henkel was not at home; a nephew let the detectives in. As they queried the nephew about his uncle's whereabouts, the detectives noticed small scraps of paper attached by magnets to the door of the refrigerator. Before they could examine the reminders more carefully, Henkel arrived and threw a fit. He screamed for the detectives to leave.

Henkel had not arrived soon enough.

Although the detectives left more quickly than they had wanted, they still had seen a couple messages on the fridge. One read, "Call Jack in California."

Meanwhile Detectives Payne and Lackovic began to learn more about the woman whose butchered body had been found in the airport motel.

Deborah Gentile was a hard-luck character. She dropped out of high school at age seventeen after getting pregnant. The much older man married her, but left two years later.

After her divorce, she began one of the few careers open to dropouts from Lawrenceville with little opportunity for anything else. She started tending bar and waiting on tables. Then one day she met Henkel, her killer. Months before her death, she moved to the small southern California town of Whittier to manage a jewelry business that the FBI said was owned by Jack Siggson, the Philadelphia con and close associate of the Hallmark Gang, the "Jack" on the deadly little refrigerator memo.

About four months after the killing, the messages on the fridge became of even greater interest to the two detectives when a representative for Lee Management, Inc., called on behalf of the Airline Passenger Association.

During his three years on the homicide squad, Payne already had learned to respect the role that fate plays in an investigation. As tenacious an investigator as he was, the com-

pactly built six-year-veteran cop knew that
sometimes tenacity just wasn't enough to
solve a case. He had seen his share of "easy"
cases from handling barroom killings in the
Mon Valley and domestic slayings in the
South Hills. A detective almost seemed irrel-
evant in those kinds of killings, since the suspect often never even left the scene.

But the Gentile case was different. There
were no witnesses, and no solid suspects.

His instinct pointed to Henkel as the
killer, but Payne had few leads to turn his gut
feeling into an arrest.

As so often happens in complex investigations, the call from Lois Lee of Lee Management was the big break. It helped Payne
accelerate the probe.

Lee Management handled insurance claims
and customer service for the Airline Passenger Association, an organization of frequent
fliers.

One of APA's services was flight insurance.

"It's a truly unique, low-cost insurance
plan," Lois Lee told Payne. As she explained,
the Texas company had an arrangement with
Lloyds of London that enabled APA to sell
insurance at one penny a week for every one
thousand dollars of coverage. APA advertised
its insurance as a way "to give you peace of
mind."

And it not only gave your loved ones finan

cial security in the event of your demise in a crash, it also covered your permanent checkout at airport terminals.

Lee told Payne and his partner that she was calling because someone had filed a claim against a life insurance policy that Gentile had purchased less than two months before her death. The first letter from the beneficiary was dated exactly one month after Gentile had been killed. Lee Management sent a claim form and asked the claimant to fill it out. It was returned three months later.

Normally, Lee explained, there would be no problem with the claim, but this one was somewhat troubling since it did involve a homicide. Moreover, as Lee explained, the beneficiary was not related to the dearly departed.

The beneficiary was a little old lady—Hannah Henkel, mother of Debbie Gentile's friend, Richie.

The insurance rep also said that Gentile had mailed the application in March, 1979, and that it apparently was from an ad run in "Ambassador," the TWA flight magazine. Although most everything else on the application was in Gentile's handwriting, the words "Hannah Henkel" were typed in the blank space marked "beneficiary."

This was all very interesting, the detectives thought. But what really startled them was the value that Gentile had placed on her life, eight hundred thousand dollars—a heck of a lot more than she could afford in premiums, even cheap ones.

The detectives were told one other significant thing about the application. It asked that the original policy be sent to Gentile in care of Jack Siggson Jewelry, Inc.

Payne smiled. He and his partner Lackovic would be heading out to California.

There, he and Lackovic spent a month looking for Siggson—and, with him, the key police needed to solve a long list of open murder cases.

*   *   *

When their main evidence in a case comes from the mouth of an informant who is almost as dirty as the defendant, prosecutors often tell juries that the only way police can break a conspiracy is to rely on one of the plotters, no matter how distasteful it might seem.

In the case of the Commonwealth versus Richard Henkel, Jack Siggson was as distasteful a government witness as had ever made a deal to save his own skin.

Like many informants who are inconvenienced to do one good thing for society on occasion, Siggson was otherwise worthless.

When he walked, you looked for a trail of slime.

Thirty-eight years old in 1980, Siggson looked ten years older. Slightly overweight and balding, he wore wide-lensed, smoked glasses that intensified his ugly demeanor. And, when he began to talk about his underworld activities, it was clear he had concern for no one on earth other than Jack Siggson.

The Philadelphia native often said that he got mixed up with Henkel because he was afraid not to. Yet, Siggson's rap sheet also showed he didn't avoid the profit.

He operated on the fringes of the Mafia. In 1968, he was charged with shooting an underworld infidel outside a northern New Jersey tavern. When he gave himself up a few days after a warrant was issued, Siggson was accompanied by a lawyer considered the mouthpiece for the Genovese crime family in New York City. Although sentenced to a twelve-to-eighteen-year prison term for that killing, Siggson was out on the streets by 1973. He soon fell in with the infamous Hallmark Gang.

Siggson met Henkel through Hallmark Gang leader Louis Kripplebauer, who eventually received ten consecutive life terms in prison for the North Carolina burglaries.

Siggson said he actually was never introduced to Henkel, but—like two ordinary businessmen—they bumped into each other at Greater Pitt airport in 1976; Henkel was picking up two ounces of heroin that Siggson agreed to transport for Kripplebauer on a flight from Philadelphia.

In no time, the two hit it off. Soon, Siggson and Henkel were fencing stolen jewelry in Florida and California. They did so well that they started their own gold and jewelry business in California as a front for the operation. And when the partners opened shop in 1979, their only employee was Deborah Gentile.

When they first confronted Siggson, the two homicide detectives almost immediately suspected he knew more about his employee's demise than he wanted to talk about. He told them Debbie had flown to Pittsburgh the day before her body had been found and that he had no idea why she went there. As hard as the detectives tried to shake his story, Siggson wouldn't budge.

After they had returned to Pittsburgh to continue their investigation, Payne and Lackovic eventually were able to "flip" the elusive jeweler with the help of what already had become a powerful weapon for local law enforcement officials in Allegheny County—the grand jury.

Like its federal counterpart, the county grand jury enabled prosecutors and police to do things that detectives had been unable to do through conventional means. Through the panel, they could subpoena records from banks and other institutions that normally protected an individual's private life from official scrutiny.

More importantly, detectives could force reluctant witnesses to testify by having them brought before a grand jury under a grant of immunity. Once immunized from prosecution on the basis of anything they said, a witness had to testify or face an indefinite jail term for contempt. If a witness lied, perjury charges could be filed as well.

Patrick J. Thomassey, a tenacious prosecutor with a boyish face and a hot Italian temper who had worked with the panel that unraveled the Manpower mess, was still assigned to the grand jury when Payne and Lackovic turned to it for help in cracking the Gentile homicide. For the remaining half of 1979, the detectives and Thomassey used the grand jury to chase a paper trail showing Gentile's movements for the last few days of her life.

Through witnesses as well as telephone records and other documents, Thomassey and the two detectives had been able to show the grand jury that Gentile flew to Pittsburgh the day before she died.

She seemed to have been on a mission that had something to do with Siggson and Henkel. Police knew that four days before her body was found, Gentile had a thirty-one-minute phone conversation with someone at Henkel's townhouse.

They also knew that she had told a cousin she was going to be meeting Siggson on the morning of May 17, hours before she took the afternoon flight to Pittsburgh, and that the meeting had something to do with a secret job Henkel wanted her to perform. The grand jury also had heard testimony indicating that Gentile probably didn't know she was going to Pittsburgh as a result of that Siggson meeting: She had talked to friends both in Pittsburgh and in California over the last few days of her life and never mentioned any trip. She also had made plans to be with a friend on the evening of May 18 on the West Coast. Moreover, her ticket for the flight had been purchased—in cash—less than an hour before she boarded the plane.

By the time that the grand jury was scheduled in February, 1980, to hear from Jack Siggson, the panel had good reason to believe that he was one of the last acquaintances to see Gentile alive and that he knew full well why Gentile had made an apparently unplanned flight across the continent less than twenty-four hours before her death.

But Siggson stuck with the same story he had told Lackovic and Payne months earlier. That story prompted the grand jury to declare that "Siggson's false explanation of his and Ms. Gentile's activities has influenced, impeded, and dissuaded this grand jury from pursuing its investigation." It recommended charges of perjury and false swearing.

Thomassey was only too willing to oblige. A warrant was issued for the arrest of Siggson. By this time, Siggson had gone underground with his wife and baby. But it didn't take California police too long to track him down and throw him in jail to await extradition.

Thomassey hoped that Siggson wouldn't fight extradition. In fact, he was hoping that he wouldn't even have to prosecute Siggson for lying.

When he flew to California, Thomassey had a different plan: persuade Siggson to testify about the death of Gentile and what detectives believed was the role that Henkel played in that homicide.

Siggson didn't need much persuasion. By then, he was convinced that he needed to be saved from the fate that so often came to Henkel's shrinking circle of friends.

Siggson began to sing.

And his first song was all about how Debbie Gentile was set up for a rendezvous with death.

But there was much more newsy stuff—he lowered the boom on Thomassey: "You'll be next," Siggson told the assistant DA.

* * *

Deborah Gentile died as she had lived:

She was the perfect patsy for a narcissist who needed no degree in psychology to be able to persuade cons to take the blame for his crimes, to persuade friends to commit crimes, and, as Gentile's own murder demonstrated, even to persuade women to take out life insurance on themselves for him.

Gentile had the fatal misfortune of knowing someone who was an actuary's worst nightmare, a hardened killer who, as police eventually learned, had nearly perfected the art of murder for insurance.

Worse yet for her life expectancy, Gentile was under the thumb of this man. She became the big score for a thug who believed that the only good ex-friend was a dead ex-friend.

For Henkel, ex-friends were tickets to a quick buck.

"I don't think he had any friends," Siggson said. "He once told me he liked me as much as he liked Gary Small or anybody else, but that 'If anybody offered me money to kill you, I'd kill you.'"

He said Henkel paused and said, "But I wouldn't hurt you." Siggson naturally found little comfort in what Henkel undoubtedly considered words of reassurance.

Recalling that chilling conversation, Siggson said that maybe there were a few people on earth whom Henkel wouldn't harm. "He said the only people he cared about was his family, and that as far as anybody else was concerned, they were fair game."

Gentile became fair game about two years after she met Henkel through their mutual companion, Sue Dixon, the girl who ended up in a trunk in New Ken in 1978. In 1977, Gentile needed a job and Henkel hired her to manage Jeff's Bar, a dive in which he had a piece of the action on Pittsburgh's West End. For a time, Henkel even let Gentile stay with him and Sue. When Sue died in mid-1978, Henkel moved to a townhouse without Gentile. And by late 1978, Henkel became fed up for some reason with Gentile. So he had her fired from Jeff's Bar, throwing her into one of the most rugged periods of her life of misfortune.

The grand jury later said that the first three months of Gentile's final year on earth were the worst of her life. She was hounded by bill collectors and beset by other severe personal problems.

Then, in early March of 1979, she started thinking things were going to change. They did, all right, but not for the better.

Henkel surprised her with a telephone call and offered her a new job. He explained that he and Siggson had opened up a jewelry shop and that she would be perfect to "watch over our interests." Gentile jumped at the chance, flew to California and deposited two hundred dollars—all that she had left—in a checking account.

Siggson, too, was surprised when Henkel called him with word of their new employee. "I don't think he even gave me her name," he later testified. "He told me to hire her. 'Just do me a favor and I'll explain it to you later on,' he told me. When I told him I didn't have anything for her to do, he said, 'Let her help your wife.'"

Siggson learned the reason for Henkel's sudden generosity when he picked him up at the Anaheim, California, airport a few days after the girl had flown in.

"He had a couple of forms with him from an insurance company and said he ran across a plan when he was in Florida. He said insurance companies are the best way in the world to make money," Siggson said.

When the two men met up with her, Henkel told Gentile, "Let's fill these forms out for Mom."

"Dick made one out on himself, but then threw it away," Siggson recalled. "He gave me the form Debbie had filled out and told me to hold on to it until he told me what to do with it later. A few days after, he gave me one thousand dollars cash, three hundred forty for the policy, plus two thousand dollars for me for her salary. He said he was going to have her killed for the eight-hundred-thousand-dollar policy."

Later, Henkel asked Gentile for a check for three hundred forty dollars.

"By that time I don't think she even remembered that form she filled out. He told me to take the check and the form and type his mother's name out on it 'so that it's nice and clear.' "

After Gentile received the policy, Siggson asked if he could hold it overnight. His instructions were to send it to Henkel because "he wanted to see the wording of the policy." When Debbie asked, a week later, what happened to the policy, Siggson told her that his baby daughter had gotten hold of it and destroyed it, and that he had sent away for another copy. "I knew Dick was going to kill her and wanted the paperwork," he later recalled.

Siggson said Henkel often told him that "he hated her guts," although he never understood why. "He was nice to her on the surface when she was around him," he said. And she was extremely loyal to Henkel. "Everything I would say to her, she would report to Dick," Siggson said.

To those who knew her, that came as no

shock. Gentile had a reputation as a "motor-mouth"—a distinct liability for someone who had been close to a man who thought nothing of killing talkers who could put him back in prison.

Siggson waffled between sympathy for the target of Henkel's get-rich-quick brainstorm and concern for his own hide. Ultimately, he simply resolved his dilemma in the same way he resolved other decisions in his life: He looked out for himself.

He said he tried acting hostile toward Gentile in the hope she would quit and disappear before Henkel could implement his insurance plan. "I would tell her to get out and a few hours later I'd get a call from Dick. He'd ask if I was trying to foul him up.

"She wasn't there to really work. She was there for another purpose. I knew what was in store for her. I tried to tell her indirectly, but every time I said something, she just told Dick. Finally I said to myself that if she won't listen, it was her tough luck."

Moreover, Siggson conceded, after a while he didn't have to feign dislike for Debbie. "She was not the easiest person to like. I didn't care what happened to her. Still," Siggson said, "it bothered me whenever I saw her," because he knew what lay ahead.

On the fifth last day of Gentile's life, Henkel called from a pay phone—Siggson said he always was using pay phones to call out to

California—and told him that he wanted Gentile to come back to Pittsburgh.

"He gave me times and an airline, but told me not to tell her she was going until she got to the house the day she was leaving. He also told me I should drive her to the airport. He told me to make sure she flew at night and was very emphatic that she leave on May 17. He said he was going to have her killed and resolve the matter of this insurance."

Siggson said Henkel "felt Pittsburgh was the best place to kill her because he could control the situation better." Henkel also wanted to keep her in the dark about her trip until the last minute to make sure she would not tell anyone she was flying to Pittsburgh to meet him. That part of Henkel's plan helped trip him up with the grand jury investigating Gentile's death. Since friends and relatives testified that Gentile never told them about her trip, prosecutor Thomassey was able to use that fact as corroboration for Siggson's testimony.

When Gentile appeared at his home on May 17, Siggson told her she had to fly to Pittsburgh. Debbie never complained that she had no change of clothes to fly across the continent. But, Siggson recalled, "She seemed a little stunned."

In a matter of moments, he knew why.

"She turned and looked at me and said, 'If I go to Pittsburgh, Dick will kill me.' "

Siggson said he asked Debbie why she was going if she feared for her life. All she replied was, "I have to go." Siggson shook his head, and drove her to the airport.

Siggson said that as Debbie purchased her ticket, "I stayed away from the ticket counter so that no one would remember me." At the same time, he didn't stray too far because "Mr. Henkel told me to stay with her so she wouldn't make any phone calls. She seemed a little scared, but she was more scared of Dick than anyone else.

"When I walked away as she boarded, I was hoping she would turn back and walk away," Siggson continued. "That way, this whole matter would be resolved. All Dick's plans would have been fouled up. You hope sometimes a situation will go away, but often it doesn't."

Siggson then made sure this situation would not "go away."

Following instructions he got days before, he walked to a phone booth and called Henkel to tell him that his mark was on her way.

It didn't take long for Siggson to learn that Debbie's premonition was correct. While Allegheny County detectives were foraging for clues around her corpse, Henkel was ten miles away in another telephone booth calling his West Coast partner.

"He told me she was killed," Siggson testified. "Who actually killed her, I do not know. He told me he was responsible for her death, for the insurance policy, and that he had a good, airtight alibi. He always seems to be on vacation when anything happens to anybody."

Siggson said he again asked Henkel why he had Gentile killed in Pittsburgh. "He said Pittsburgh was his home and he knew it best."

Two months later, Henkel told him he thought the insurance company was close to settling. But even if the firm balked, Henkel "said that if they don't pay off in this one, he had a husband and wife lined up."

Although Henkel promised him fifty thousand dollars for his help in setting up Gentile, Siggson claimed he didn't do it for the money. "Knowing Mr. Henkel and his business, I knew what his plans were and that if I didn't go along, I'd be dead," he explained.

Less than a year later, Siggson began getting the strange feeling that he was about to be dead anyway.

\* \* \*

By early 1980, Thomassey, Payne, Lackovic, and the grand jury were slowly closing in.

Henkel knew it, too.

Many of his associates who had been subpoenaed before the grand jury told him the
nature of the panel's questions. Later, witnesses said that Henkel on at least two occasions talked of sending Thomassey a bomb.

Henkel also helped some witnesses who
had been subpoenaed by the grand jury that
was hot on his trail. He accompanied Small
during the Edgewood cop's appearance before the grand jury. And he coached Siggson
in elaborate detail, putting a little muscle behind his words of advice.

"With most of my testimony, before I went
to appear, Mr. Henkel went over what I
would say," Siggson recalled, adding that by
July, 1980, Henkel began losing confidence
in mere coaching.

Siggson recalled that federal agents
warned him that he was a marked man. One
FBI agent "told me Mr. Henkel was coming
to California and they had reason to believe
my life was in danger. They wanted to have
an agent with me as close by as possible
when I met him because they felt strongly
he was going to kill me."

As the pressure grew, Siggson didn't know
where to turn. After the grand jury recommended his prosecution for perjury, he continued meeting Henkel, who "told me not to
worry."

Yet, during those meetings, Siggson said,
"I thought he had a more permanent solution

in mind. He told me, 'If you're not with me, I'll do a complete genocide on your family. I'll kill everybody.' "

Terrified by the prospect that Henkel was about to shrink his circle of friends further, Siggson sold his house and moved to another town where he lived until his perjury arrest.

With Siggson's testimony in hand, Thomassey and the two homicide detectives finally moved in on their quarry.

On October 22, 1980, the grand jury unanimously recommended Henkel's prosecution on first degree murder for the motel slaying.

The next day, with the secret presentment locked in a judge's safe, more than two dozen county police and FBI agents—now the feds surfaced—staged a predawn strike at Henkel's townhouse in Hampton.

When they broke down the door, Richie Henkel momentarily lost the ice-cold composure that terrorized his friends and enemies alike.

Startled by the door being kicked open, Henkel lost control of his sphincter muscle.

As the law enforcement agents waited for Henkel to clean up, some of the detectives began foraging through his townhouse. They found electronic gear, tapes, and a gun registered to the Edgewood cop.

They also found another piece in the complex circumstantial case they were weaving to try to send Henkel to the electric chair.

Stuffed in a dresser drawer was a will in which Hannah Henkel left all her possessions to her son Richard, to the exclusion of two other sons.

The will was dated May 17, 1979, the same day Debbie Gentile began her airplane trip to the grave.

The discovery prompted Payne to recall Siggson's account of Henkel's devotion to his family. Mom was high on the list of favorite relatives.

* * *

Standing in a dark blue sweatsuit wearing handcuffs and leg irons on the morning of his arrest, Henkel glared at Common Pleas Judge Robert E. Dauer as the charges were read.

Henkel was furious. He ranted at the judge that he had been arrested as a publicity scheme, that his name had been dragged through the mud by an ambitious assistant district attorney.

Dauer patiently listened to the tirade, then asked Thomassey for a recommendation on bail.

Henkel said nothing when Thomassey replied that no bail should be granted because this was a case for capital punishment.

Henkel claimed to have no money of his

own—an assertion that police were unable to dispute since they couldn't get a search warrant for Hannah Henkel's home in Youngstown, where they thought he stashed a fortune in stolen jewelry and cash. So when Henkel told Dauer that he could not afford his own lawyer, the judge appointed one of the county's most flamboyant attorneys to represent him.

Some courthouse observers were surprised when unorthodox Paul Gettleman appeared as counsel. Henkel was not the poor ghetto dweller that Gettleman often was commanded to represent at public expense. Somehow, Gettleman's nearly waist-length, braided pony tail and wardrobe of combat boots and jeans fit with black clients from poverty areas. But this time it was incongruous.

Nevertheless, Gettleman pursued the case with the same obstinacy and fervor that he provided to poor blacks. He demanded grand jury transcripts—a move Thomassey vehemently denounced because he feared that would endanger witnesses, especially since he and detectives believed that Henkel had allies on the street who shared his homicidal tendencies.

Although Henkel and Gettleman lost that round, the defense attorney filed a slew of other motions in an attempt to derail the

case. Gettleman claimed it was based solely
on questionable circumstantial evidence and
the testimony of an admitted perjurer. Henkel also began reading law books, apparently
discarding his pursuit of a psychology degree.

In late 1980, police and prosecutors gave
Gettleman yet another case to worry about,
striking at Henkel and three of his followers
with another bombshell charge.

They accused Henkel of plotting to kidnap
prominent Pittsburghers with the aid of Star
Wars technology that astonished even veteran technicians at the U.S. Bureau of Alcohol, Tobacco, and Firearms. The scheme
itself was also astonishing: blow up the hostages if a one-million-dollar ransom was not
produced.

Had the plans come off, the first target
would have been more likely to earn Henkel
a death sentence from a Pittsburgh jury than
six Deborah Gentiles. They planned to ab-
duct Pittsburgh Steelers owner Art Rooney,
Sr. But they dropped that idea when they figured his weak heart would give out under
the stress. Their next target, whom they
stalked for several days, was Edward M.
Ryan of Washington County, the founder and
president of Ryan Homes, Inc., the nation's
third largest builder of single-family dwell-
ings in the suburbs.

The plot called for ambushing the victims with the aid of space-age devices designed by Roy Travis, Henkel's onetime cellmate at the Marion federal penitentiary, the electronics whiz from Vancouver. The gadgets relied on radio waves to disengage an automobile ignition system while the car was moving. Although detectives initially reacted with skepticism when they heard Siggson describe the plan, they believed him once they found the devices in Henkel's townhouse and were told by ATF technicians that the things actually worked during field tests.

Once they had their victim, the conspirators planned to tie a remote-controlled bomb around his waist and stick him in a van loaded with five-gallon containers of gasoline. Then they would force the victim to call someone who could pay the ransom. They would monitor the conversation through an electronic bugging device planted in the van. The bug would enable them to eavesdrop on both sides of the conversation.

Initially, as Siggson explained to detectives and the grand jury, Henkel had hoped to pull off the first kidnapping in 1977. Among his co-conspirators were Officer Small, Travis, Gentile, Sue Dixon, Hallmark Gang members Bruce Agnew and Louis Kripplebauer, and Siggson himself. Siggson told police that Small and Henkel would take dynamite out to abandoned lots far away from Pittsburgh and detonate them with remote-control devices to make sure they were hooked up right. The conspiracy was dormant while Henkel pondered substitute targets; Ryan had been dropped from the eligibility list when no one could figure out what he looked like.

Although the conspiracy was never fully implemented, prosecutors had sufficient evidence to charge Henkel and several of his friends.

With the help of the grand jury and Siggson's testimony in the investigation, detectives arrested Small, Kripplebauer, Henkel, and Travis. But the ensuing legal machinations were almost as complex and bizarre as the crime.

A judge ruled that the legal papers filed by prosecutors to effect the foursome's arrest were improperly drawn up, forcing the district attorney into an appeal that took months to resolve. Meanwhile, Travis' extradition from Canada became mired in international paperwork because the Canadian government found the entire case preposterous. The district attorney's office obtained the aid of the U.S. State Department in an effort to resolve the dispute. But even Uncle Sam couldn't help, and Travis was never extradited.

Ironically, the Canadian government also

turned away the help that homicide detectives Payne and Lackovic had offered in linking Travis to the unsolved 1975 bombing death of the Vancouver restaurateur who died when he opened a Pittsburgh-postmarked package. The shrapnel in that bomb was identical to the washer-and-nail mix in the bomb that killed masseuse Sasha Scott. Moreover, Payne identified the photo of the woman who had mailed the package from the branch post office in Oakland as Sue Dixon. Further linking Travis to the crime was the fact that the package actually had been addressed to the victim's son, a department store security guard whose testimony in a shoplifting incident involving Travis could have sent Henkel's onetime federal cellmate back to jail.

Even before the kidnapping charges were filed against him, Small also began seeing his ten-year career as an Edgewood cop unravel with Henkel's arrest in the Gentile case.

The discovery in Henkel's home of a 9-millimeter pistol registered to Small and a similar discovery in the home of a Youngstown hitman named Joseph DeRose threw Edgewood officials into a panic. Things like this, they thought, might happen in neighboring Wilkinsburg, but Edgewood?

DeRose was a professional killer allied with a crime family headed by Ronald "The Crab" Carabbia, a lieutenant in a Mafia faction of Cleveland mobster James Licavoli. At the time that Small's weapon was found in DeRose's home, Youngstown was in the throes of an old-fashioned gangland war between Carabbia's family and one headed by Joseph Naples, an associate of then-Western Pennsylvania Mafia godfather John LaRocca.

In 1977, Carabbia was convicted of the car-bombing death of a Cleveland racketeer who had been at odds with Licavoli. Carabbia's imprisonment, in turn, started a fight for Youngstown between the LaRocca and Licavoli clans. DeRose was considered to have played a major role in some of the eight gangland killings that occurred between 1978 and 1979 as an outgrowth of that dispute.

In fact, police theorized that Henkel himself had been involved in some of those executions.

Police found Small's gun in DeRose's home as the result of a botched hit. As DeRose was unlocking the front door to his house, someone in a passing auto fired three shots. One wounded the target. Police arrived and searched DeRose's home, discovering the Edgewood cop's piece. For his part, DeRose wasn't talking.

By 1981, he wasn't anywhere to be found, either. In February, 1981, DeRose's father was shotgunned to death. Two months later, police found the younger DeRose's car, unoccupied and burning, in Niles, Ohio, near Youngstown.

DeRose himself was never located, but police figured he finally fell victim to his underworld enemies. For a time in 1980, DeRose had managed to successfully avoid those enemies: He was hiding out in Henkel's Hampton townhouse. Once Henkel was arrested in the Gentile murder, DeRose returned to Ohio.

With Henkel's arrest in the Gentile case, Small's murky associations with shaky individuals and known felons became a matter of public knowledge. Edgewood officials acted as quickly as they could to stop the bad publicity.

The mayor and borough council first suspended Small and later dismissed him from the force for conduct unbecoming an officer. It was no great loss in terms of a personnel shortage. Small had a history of taking off long periods of time on disability for a back injury he supposedly sustained while on duty.

In addition to the kidnap-bomb-plot charges, Small also was arrested on federal charges of giving known felons firearms. Eventually, he was acquitted of the firearms charge and won a dismissal of the kidnapping case. Then, he moved to Okinawa, Japan, where he secured a civilian job with the U.S.

Army that kept him in close proximity to lots of firearms.

In 1988, Small sued Edgewood over his dismissal, seeking three hundred thousand dollars in back pay. During a civil service commission hearing, Siggson and homicide detectives testified about the guns and the kidnapping case. The three-member civil service commission heard that Small was the conspirator who was to subdue the kidnap targets. The panel was told of tape recordings of instructions on using the car-crippling and eavesdropping devices that had been mailed to Small's home. It learned that two of his guns had been found in the homes of less-than-respectable citizens.

The panel declared, "We find that Small was engaged in an extortion plot and knew that Richard Henkel, a convicted felon, had engaged in criminal activity by possessing a firearm owned by Small." It turned down Small's request for back pay. He has appealed that decision to state courts.

Along with Small's gun, Hannah Henkel's will, and the gadgets that were to be used in the kidnapping plot, detectives found other incriminating items in Henkel's home. One of the most bizarre was a lease he had obtained only a few months before his arrest for an office in the Clark Building, not far from the massage parlors.

Detectives searched the office and made a chilling discovery.

There were no furnishings, not even a fern. But there were four gasmasks hidden above a panel of the ceiling. That prompted investigators to wonder if Henkel had been planning some kind of daring holdup of the gem merchants in the Clark Building, the diamond row of the Golden Triangle.

Henkel wasn't saying anything. Denied bond because Thomassey had singled him out for the death penalty, he stewed in jail while boning up on criminal law and procedure. In 1981, his brother Robert and a former city fireman who owned Jeff's Bar were arrested for plotting Henkel's escape. Although Henkel was not charged in the plot, detectives had no doubt that he was in on the pre-trial plan for freedom. Witnesses recalled that an inmate charged in the plot, James "Sonny" Watson, had been seen having numerous conversations with Henkel in the County Jail.

Watson was well known to detectives, and not just because he was awaiting trial for murder.

His notoriety dated back several years in West Virginia where he castrated himself so he could be moved from prison to a mental hospital, and then he tried to break out of it.

As months dragged on, the Gentile case became tied in pre-trial knots. Finally, in April, 1983, it appeared the pre-trial foot-dragging was drawing to an end.

And that's when Richard Henkel made the jailbird's equivalent of a football quarterback's "Hail Mary" pass.

On April 14, 1983, Henkel was in Western Penitentiary preparing for a routine strip search before he boarded a sheriff's van bound for the Allegheny County Courthouse. Only a few months earlier, he had wrangled a transfer from the county jail to the big house on the Ohio River by complaining that conditions in the local lockup were violating his Constitutional rights. With him that morning was a 26-year-old Scranton punk named Dennis Coviello, who was scheduled to testify on Henkel's behalf in a pre-trial hearing.

Just as Henkel was ready to begin removing his clothes, he lifted his shoe and pulled out two small derringers that had been hidden in a hollowed heel. Smuggled into the prison by a guard, the guns enabled Henkel and Coviello to take another guard, Dennis Kohut, and civilian records keeper, Gus Mastros, hostage.

The huge gate at the prison door slammed shut before Henkel and Coviello could exit. Panicked, they pulled their two hostages into a small commissary room. For the next two days, they said nothing. As reporters waited in the wind-whipped, icy rain, and state troopers toted shotguns and stood patiently on the inside perimeter of Western Pen, Henkel and Coviello grew increasingly more desperate as each hour of the five-day siege passed.

Over eavesdropping equipment that had been installed in vents leading to the room, law enforcement officials listened as Henkel screamed threats at his captives, threats to kill them slowly.

Six days after the attempted escape began, Henkel and Coviello gave up.

Although Mastros, a slightly built man, eventually returned to work at Western Pen, the strapping guard, Kohut, retired on permanent disability. His nerves were shattered by the experience of having Henkel put a revolver to his head, playing Russian roulette. Months after the episode ended, Kohut would wander into the fourth-floor newsroom in the Allegheny County Courthouse to tell the story. As he greeted them, reporters who once had clamored to interview him now backed away. He was a broken man, but by then they were chasing other stories. He was old news.

In January, 1984, Henkel was taken to Philadelphia to stand trial for the Gentile murder. He had been granted a change of venue as a result of the publicity from the hostage siege at Western Pen.

Before a jury was picked, Henkel stunned prosecutors and police with an offer to make a deal.

Henkel decided to plead guilty to the Gentile murder in return for a promise that he would receive a life sentence instead of the electric chair. He agreed to plead guilty because he wanted to spare his brother Robert a prison term. Shortly before Richie's trial, Robert was convicted of a firearms charge in connection with the escape attempt in 1981 at the Allegheny County Jail that involved Watson, the self-made eunuch.

Because his brother faced certain jail, Richie bartered for probation. He got the deal by offering detectives something that they felt was well worth probation for brother Robert.

Richie agreed to plead guilty to four other homicides, resolving once and for all what the "massage parlor war" was really all about.

\*   \*   \*

The killer and the coterie of his pursuers barely had unpacked their bags in Philadelphia in January, 1984, when Henkel's startling decision had them all headed back to Pittsburgh.

There they consummated a deal that took Henkel off the streets for good. No death penalty, true. But no more chances for early release, either. He was going away for five consecutive life terms, with no hope for conning prison officials or judges with back-to-school ruses.

The cops got most of what they wanted. The fierce pre-trial maneuvering now was reduced to putting the finishing touches on an arrangement that would put Henkel away for good.

But many of the mysteries unearthed by police in the wake of their pursuit of Deborah Gentile's killer never were solved, such was the clever way that Henkel arranged his plea non-bargain.

He provided some details to two killings, elaborate information about two others, and simply acknowledged that the case against him in a fifth was true. Henkel had the last laugh, though, because he was able to leave the detectives with many unanswered questions.

The big question, of course, was answered:

The massage parlor war never existed. Before the publicity had died down to a trickle, the phantom conflict had served some useful purpose. Some Pittsburgh officials used the killings to turn up the volume of public pressure on dens of iniquity that operated boldly in the city. That pressure caused the rub joints some harm, but changing tastes and lifestyles virtually killed them off; they faded away because their customers had drifted off.

As for the victims who initially were counted as casualties in the make-believe war, only the slaying of rub joint kingpin George Lee in 1975 remains unsolved.

Some police privately suggested that the massage parlor war was an artful Henkel ruse, a connivance to throw suspicion from himself by making it appear as if racket bosses were fighting. He was so cunning, so deliberate, so twisted that he would resort to blowing a masseuse to smithereens and get a good laugh while reporters and cops speculated about an underworld skirmish.

Two of the five killings to which Henkel confessed were unrelated to the "massage parlor war." During his interrogation and guilty plea, he carefully omitted details that would put some allies in the jackpot with him, just in case he needed them.

Nonetheless, his confessions and the evidence that was gathered independently during the long investigation of the "massage parlor war" helped police understand the real reason why Sasha and Glenn Scott, Sue

Dixon, and Debbie Gentile had died—insurance payoffs. Henkel profited handsomely from those killings—and he eliminated potentially vexatious witnesses as a fringe benefit.

The same held true for the victims police didn't even know about until the Gentile homicide probe was well underway.

Consider, for example, the case of Lawrence Windsor, the never-found partner in the bank robbery that netted Henkel his first serious jail time—Henkel's prerehabbilitation era.

Just before Henkel staged his dramatic hostage siege at Western Pen, homicide detectives received a letter from Windsor's daughter. Heidi Carter wanted them to help arrange a meeting between her and Henkel so that she could find out what really happened to her dad.

Then 20, Heidi was desperate to learn what transpired when she was just a baby in 1969. She had grown up in Churchill with the knowledge only that her father had died. More recently she had learned that her father's actual fate remained unknown.

Why she even cared was a puzzle. Police thought Windsor was hardly worth missing. His wife testified in a hearing on her petition to have him declared dead that he often beat her, gambled away paychecks, and cared little for their asthmatic daughter. Oddly, Windsor's widow failed to persuade the judge that she was entitled to that death declaration, even though her lawyer had argued that her husband's association with Henkel constituted being in the presence of a known peril. Henkel could fool some judges even without lifting a finger.

Heidi sought to fill a void in her personal history. When Henkel finally ended his hostage stand-off, she wrote letters imploring him to let her visit. She just needed to know, she wrote, if her father had been killed. She didn't want a share of the loot, just the truth about her dad.

The wily, sadistic killer never answered her.

But several years after Henkel had been put away, Heidi received a mysterious letter from the state prison in Graterford, near Philadelphia. It was signed by James Watson. Watson's letter told Heidi that for ten thousand dollars he would tell her what happened to her father, and he instructed her to make arrangements to call the warden at Graterford and set up a phone call between him and her.

Was the sadistic psychologist Henkel at work again?

Married, pregnant with twins, and finally settling down in life, Heidi went nearly hysterical. She had put her father out of her mind for more than two years and, suddenly, those unanswered questions had come back to haunt her. Heidi called Payne in a panic. He and Lackovic went to Graterford after telling Heidi to play along with Watson.

Typical of someone who would remove his own testicles, Watson was too short-sighted to consider that the line might be tapped when Heidi's call was made. After recording the call, prison authorities busted Watson. But he never would tell whether Henkel had inspired the cruel hoax.

Police had reason to count Windsor among Henkel's chain of presumed dead. They found two witnesses who said Henkel told them that he had bludgeoned Windsor with a hammer, then dumped the body in quicklime to avoid detection.

They also had witnesses who were prepared to testify that Henkel probably did the same thing to James Barone, another missing con.

Barone was a co-defendant with Henkel in another bank heist in 1969. Although both men pleaded guilty to burglarizing the bank, Barone never showed up for sentencing. More than one hundred thirty-three thousand dollars in cash, bonds, and money orders never was recovered.

Moreover, Barone also was an informant for the U.S. Secret Service in connection with a counterfeiting investigation that involved Henkel. Barone's disappearance eliminated any chance that Henkel would have to worry about going to jail for that caper.

As Henkel learned that police had witnesses who could tie him to crimes such as Barone and Windsor vanishing, he became nearly ill with fear in the weeks before his scheduled trial. One reason he staged the foiled escape from Western Pen was because the prosecution had lined up devastating testimony in the trial for Gentile's murder. Prosecutors planned to put witnesses on the stand to show a jury that Gentile was only the latest victim in a string of homicides committed by Henkel for the same reasons.

Although prosecutors reckoned they had insufficient evidence to charge Henkel individually with other killings, they knew they could prove the Gentile charges by bringing in circumstances of the rest.

Prosecutors planned in the Gentile trial to argue that he killed others for insurance, and that he killed still others because they knew about other crimes he had committed. With that testimony, they would then argue to a jury that Gentile was killed for both reasons, that her death was the biggest score in a bizarre pyramid scheme. Gentile's death also eliminated a potential liability in the kidnapping plan, since she knew of that conspiracy.

Gentile was no innocent bystander, but

she was worth more dead than alive to Henkel; police believe she set up Anthony "Bobby" Pugh, the massage parlor desk man.

In the days just before the Western Pen siege, Henkel became concerned that the district attorney would win court approval to tie him to killings for which he was not formally charged. He grew obsessed with the prospect that the evidence in those cases, together with Siggson's testimony, and the other compelling evidence linking him to the Gentile slaying, would be more than enough to send him to the electric chair. For a man to whom death was a good living, Henkel was petrified at the prospect of his own.

Months after the siege, that fear ultimately drove Henkel to make his deal with the government, his life spared.

As they learned from witnesses who told them of his boasts concerning Windsor's demise and his veiled suggestions about a similar fate having met Barone, police knew Henkel had looked at murder as a convenient solution to many problems. No wonder he could put messages about them on the door of his refrigerator: for Henkel, murder was as easy and as routine as buying a quart of milk.

He began looking at murder as the best way to dispose of problems before he went to prison in the Duquesne Heights bank robbery case. But after federal prison officials certified his rehabilitation in 1974, and returned him to society, Henkel looked at murder as the *only* solution.

His first confession involved the 1975 shooting death of Andy Russmann, a small-time Mon Valley hood whose body wasn't found until after Henkel showed police where he had buried it.

During his formal interrogation in a room at the Allegheny County Courthouse in January, 1984, Henkel was the vaguest in describing Russmann's slaying. "I just helped bury Russmann," he told detectives. "Andy was going south on somebody with some money," Henkel said. "He was taking, pulling out money that was supposed to be paid over to other people. . . . I picked him up, took him to this location, other person come in, talked to him, shot him, wrapped him up and took him to the site."

Police suspect Russmann was killed in the basement of Edgewood Officer Gary Small's home.

Detectives found an old report showing that Small's wife once called police and said her husband had killed someone. After police were unable to find any evidence to support the woman's story, Small had her committed to a mental hospital. However, police have never had sufficient evidence to charge Small with any crime other than the kidnapping plot, which was dismissed, and the firearms count, of which he was acquitted.

Henkel helped detectives find Russmann's skeletal remains, taking them to a field near a Washington County gun club where Small often practiced target shooting.

On that site, they also found the remains of Thomas Bruce Agnew, a onetime Hallmark Gang victim who, in 1977, had jumped bond while awaiting trial in Philadelphia on a series of major burglary cases.

"I guess I met Bruce in '74–'75, somewhere in there," Henkel said. "He just came to Pittsburgh and he was doing burglaries and whatnot and I met him. And then when he was on the lam, I arranged for him to stay in the area."

Henkel said he shot Agnew on the gun club grounds. Using a .38-caliber revolver, he fired "two or three" hollow-point bullets into the back of his head while the victim faced an unidentified companion who had accompanied Henkel for the execution.

Henkel again refused to divulge many details about the killing, telling the detectives, "Can't give you the reason without involving other people." Other witnesses said Henkel considered Agnew a stoolie and that Henkel was particularly concerned that Agnew knew details of the kidnapping-bomb plot. Siggson told police that Henkel admitted the killing and that he explained, "Once you're in, you're in for good."

Police also believe that Henkel was responsible for the gangland execution of De-Marco, the onetime Court Lounge jester and career lowlife whose body was found in the trunk of his car only about a month after Gentile was slain. Police theorized that De-Marco's slaying was simply a contract killing and that Henkel got the job from drug dealers who were angry with DeMarco for stiffing them on a deal.

Of all the killings linked to Henkel, police have the clearest idea of his role in the deaths of Glenn and Sasha Scott, Sue Dixon, and Gentile. Although Henkel admitted being the actual killer in both Scott homicides, he only admitted setting up Gentile—giving police support for their theory that he had an accomplice in the executions of both Gentile and Dixon. Henkel refused to discuss Dixon's killing because the police and prosecutors refused to eliminate the possibility of a death sentence if he implicated himself.

Glenn Scott's slaying was a kind of trial run for the insurance schemes. It started out as just a contract killing for Henkel—but it inspired him to look at other ways to make murder a profitable endeavor.

As Henkel explained, Scott's wife, Sasha, wanted Glenn dead and ended up paying twenty thousand dollars—money she got from a policy that Glenn had taken out on his life when the two of them were happily married.

Sasha Scott didn't spend much time remaining the innocent daughter of a Midwestern family once she left home and moved to Pittsburgh at age sixteen. It seemed she couldn't wait to become a bad girl and have adventures.

She turned tricks as a street hooker until she met Scott, who introduced her to drugs and Franco Harris, who became the best man at their wedding.

Sasha soon sought a career in the theater, and was awarded a cameo role on Liberty Avenue stages: Her biggest act was putting her mouth over a twelve-inch cake shaped like a penis, and then she did the same thing with many a real penis belonging to spectators who applauded her sweet-tooth exhibition.

Along with her sexual appetites, another urge—to become a widow—was due to Scott using her as a punching bag, for fun.

What finally sealed Glenn Scott's doom, though, was that he had angered Henkel. Sasha moved in with Henkel and Sue Dixon. When Sue brought Sasha to Henkel's apartment in early 1975, Glenn was not far behind. He confronted Henkel in the parking lot and pulled a gun on him.

Scott later called and apologized. Henkel told detectives: "I had decided that he scared me so bad and I didn't know if he was ever going to do it again and I just thought I couldn't take a chance if he pulled a gun on me one more time. So I decided to kill him, eliminate him."

Then Henkel learned Sasha wanted her husband eliminated. In what Henkel called a "screwy" coincidence, Sasha got a social phone call while at Henkel's apartment from a contract killer. The man, whom Henkel never identified, agreed to kill Glenn in return for the insurance money that Sasha would receive for his death.

So without telling Sasha, Henkel called the hitman. It was time to cut a deal.

"I go talk to him and tell him that I was going to do it anyhow, you know," he told detectives. "And I told him that, you know, to be a race on, we might get in each other's way."

Henkel made a false peace with Glenn Scott after learning that Sasha was the beneficiary of his life insurance policy. He proposed to Sasha that she make her husband's death even more worthwhile by upping the payout on the policy. Henkel called Scott, casually asking him the name of his insurance company, explaining that his own insurance company was giving him some kind of trouble and that he wanted to look around for a new one.

"You know, he was going to be dead in a matter of . . . ," Henkel told detectives, breaking off the sentence. "I had no problem when he was going to die. I mean, it (the insurance) was just like a bonus on the guy."

But Sasha and Dixon blew the chances of increasing the value of Glenn's death when they visited the insurance agent and asked how they could raise the policy value without Glenn knowing about it. The agent didn't buy Sasha's explanation that she wanted to surprise her husband.

By this time, Scott himself was getting worried. He told Steeler Harris and onetime KDKA TV newscaster Dennis Holly that he was afraid he was going to be offed. He also called an FBI agent for whom he had occasionally acted as an informant and told him that he wanted to get Sasha out of prostitution, but that a guy named Dick was giving him trouble.

Still, Glenn kept trying to ingratiate himself with the man he feared. Shortly before he died in November, 1975, Glenn called Henkel and told him that he was trying to unload some rifles and pistols he had obtained from "some white kid who had done some burglaries."

Henkel arranged a meeting at Scott's stables in Richland Township, and he went there with the hitman Sasha had hired.

Detectives heard Henkel describe what happened next:

"We go into the house. Scotty takes us down to the barn. We go into this office or hardtack room, whatever they call it, where they keep bridles and saddles and stuff. The weapons were lying there. I had my gun in my waistband. Scotty turned around and I just started firing. It was eight-shot. I think it was an eight-shot (.22 caliber) pistol. I emptied it, reloaded it, and shot again. I shot him in the back of the head and as he was falling, I kept shooting him in the head. And then I think he landed on his back or something and I shot him in the eyes and ears. Most of the shots were into the head, though.

"The following days we come out to the house and Sasha took a bunch of stuff out of there then. Saddles, the whole bit. Baseball bats, records from the Manpower scandal. We kept them (the records) for a while—Sasha did. She thought they was going to be part of the estate because there was a lot of money involved there. They had two sets of books—what he was billing and what they was billing. After I saw what was going on, I destroyed them. Most of the rifles we melted down."

Two years passed and Henkel began getting bored with Sasha.

When asked to describe his relationship with her, Henkel told the detectives, "It was, like, hard to believe, like, nonexistent really. I very seldom saw Sasha at all. She would work from—no, she would get up late in the afternoon, late evenings, say five o'clock, get ready, go to work. We had hardly no relationship at all. I asked Susie, I don't know how many times, I asked her to leave. But Susie wouldn't. It was a funny arrangement. She was only supposed to stay until she got settled in and everything, but it just drug on."

It "drug on" to the point where Henkel decided to end the arrangement—and make a little money too. He persuaded Sasha to take out an eighteen-thousand-dollar life insurance policy and name Sue as her beneficiary.

In December, 1977, Henkel had several reasons to kill Sasha—"send baggage to DePaul," a reference to the coffin that carried her remains back to her hometown, was magnetized to the fridge.

"There was a rumor that Sasha had started telling people she had contracted to have Scotty killed, and I didn't know if I had any part in it," explained Henkel, who had never told Sasha that it was he, not her hired hitman, who had carried out the contract on her husband. Moreover, DeMarco, once Sasha's boss, had had a terrible argument with her over something, Henkel said.

Those two reasons, together with the insurance incentive, prompted Henkel in December, 1977, to construct the bomb. He bought a cheap alarm clock and some batteries from a drugstore for the trigger that would detonate the three sticks of dynamite and shotgun shells once the package was opened.

The alarm clock was almost too complicated a touch that could easily have killed Henkel, though he didn't realize that until Payne pointed it out during the January, 1984, confession session.

The bomb was designed to detonate when Sasha opened the box. But because he was going to have it delivered, Henkel wanted a way to delay setting the trigger until after he gave the package to a messenger. Henkel installed the alarm clock so that it would not prime the trigger until twenty minutes after he handed the package to the messenger, the taxi driver.

As complicated as his screwball plan was, it worked. Henkel tucked the bomb into a jewelry case, wrapped it, and attached a card that he designed to look like it had come from one of Sasha's lovers. Before he did all that, he worked for days on the trigger device, using a light bulb in place of the explosive to ensure that the electrical circuit was complete.

Once satisfied, he bought a Santa Claus wig and mustache and drove out to the airport. From there he called a cab to take the delivery Downtown. "I figured there was a tremendous amount of transit there, and it would be less noticeable," he said.

Henkel then went to do some Christmas shopping, confident the cab driver would never remember him because "I've worn so many disguises at different times and different places."

During his interrogation, Henkel was asked the purpose of the clock. Payne and the other detectives scratched their heads as Henkel went through a confusing explanation of his rationale for the device. If the cab driver had refused to take the package, he explained, he could return home, open the package, and use the explosive on a better idea.

Detective Payne wiped the smirk from Henkel's face when he asked, "What if Sasha didn't open it up at the Gemini Spa? You were living with her at the time. Didn't you give any thought . . . that Sasha might have taken the package home?"

"No, I never gave it any thought," Henkel replied. "I had no reason to doubt that she would open that right there after she saw the card. I knew she wouldn't have brought it home."

Payne continued: "See, most people in that situation would have a backup. You would think there would be a timing mechanism as a backup to go kaboom twenty, thirty minutes later, if it was not opened. Do you know what I'm saying?"

Henkel appeared thoughtful. Then, he said, "Should have did that, huh? Next time I'll remember that."

He also denied that the insurance policy was his major motive for killing her, insisting, "the motive was self-preservation." Of course, the money was nice, too. Another bonus for a job he felt had to be done.

Soon after the bombing, Henkel himself got a mysterious package delivered to his apartment.

Remembering his own handiwork, Henkel called a neighborhood teenager and used an excuse to get him to open it. The package was a harmless gift.

Henkel maintained that Dixon was not involved in Sasha's killing, even though she was the beneficiary of Sasha's life insurance. In fact, Henkel maintained, Dixon didn't even know he was involved in the bombing.

"Then again," he said after a pause, "she may have suspected it after Sasha was demised." Dixon knew Henkel well enough—

but, as it turned out, not well enough for her own good.

All the details surrounding Dixon's demise likely will never be unraveled. Since Henkel stopped short of giving any statement about her murder, police have no idea where she died or exactly how she was lured there.

But they are convinced that, as in the Scott murders, ample reasons existed for Henkel to want her out of the way.

Like Sasha, Dixon also came from a Catholic family and left behind the world of Baltimore Catechism almost as soon as she struck out on her own. Although her name appeared as owner on the Court Lounge's liquor license, she had been "fired" in late 1977, reportedly because she had resisted the advances of Court Lounge master-of-ceremonies DeMarco.

One source told police that she had angered DeMarco by telling him he had acquired too many bizarre tastes when he was in prison, that he only wanted to perform "back-door sex," and that he was little more than a "fag." DeMarco reportedly was enraged, but likely not half as angry as he became when he learned that she also was scheduled to testify before a federal grand jury in conjunction with an IRS probe of the Court Lounge.

The Court Lounge in reality was owned by

Anthony Repepi, the Mafia guardian of gambling operations in the southern part of Allegheny County and in much of the Mon Valley. Thus, Dixon's inability to testify before the grand jury meant a great deal to many—especially to someone like Henkel, who also sold his expertise as killer.

Police thought it no coincidence that her body was found in New Kensington just after she received a grand jury subpoena. They also believe that Henkel had her parked outside Mafia underboss Mannerino's home as a sick joke.

Dixon's death also benefitted Henkel more directly.

Only a few months before her death, she became engaged to marry Henkel. She named him heir in a will he persuaded her to draw up. She also made him the beneficiary on four life insurance policies—three of which were purchased in the six months before her death. All told, Henkel stood to make more than one hundred twenty thousand dollars from her dying.

Additionally, he stood to inherit the liquor license for the Court Lounge, which was closed by that time. The license was estimated to be worth around seventy thousand dollars because it could be used to open a saloon anywhere within Allegheny County. Most liquor licenses can be used only in the municipality or city district where the tavern for which they originally were issued is located. But this was an old license, issued when there were no geographic restrictions.

At the time of Dixon's death, the Court Lounge license was held in the office safe of Henkel's attorney, O'Hanesian, who in 1974 had argued so eloquently and persuasively on behalf of the new man—how he would never need a criminal lawyer again. It was still in that safe when Henkel again needed a criminal lawyer, big time.

Dixon's liability as a potential witness against Henkel also helped put a bull's-eye on her back. She matched the description of the woman who in 1975 had mailed the lethal package from Oakland—the bomb which blew up in Vancouver, killing the 45-year-old restaurateur who had opened it for his son, the security guard.

Dixon knew the regulars at Jeff's Bar, the West End beer garden where Henkel got a W-2 Form as manager. One regular at Jeff's was Henry "Red" Ford, a burly thug who lived upstairs. Weeks before Dixon's slaying, Ford had been released from prison after serving time for an aggravated assault conviction, the kind only a West End ruffian would admire: During a fight, Ford bit off the ear of his adversary. In 1980, Ford was again in jail awaiting trial for biting off another man's ear when charged as an accomplice in the kidnap-bomb plot.

Shortly after their daughter's death, Dixon's parents filed suit to stop Henkel from collecting on the insurance policies. They had been designated her beneficiaries originally.

With the support of his brother as an alibi, Henkel testified in a deposition that he was on the West Coast when Dixon vanished. The judge ruled against Dixon's parents, giving Henkel the money.

When they found Dixon's body, police also found a watch under the front seat of the car and traced it to Ford. Ford said Dixon borrowed it on the day she left her apartment and never returned. The police had nothing to dispute his claim.

Two years later, a grand jury asked Ford if he knew anything about the death of Deborah Gentile. No, he replied. Less than a year later, he was convicted of perjury for that single word, a giant lie.

A burning desire to solve the Dixon murder, and some of the other killings that only have been linked to Henkel, prompted detectives in 1984 to ask Henkel to return for questioning.

"I know you are giving certain things up," one detective told Henkel, "but I think maybe in your mind there is a possibility of even going further somewhere along the line."

Henkel thought for a moment before he answered, looking down at the floor. Then he glanced at Payne and pointed to the court-appointed attorney, Gettleman.

"That would be up to the counsel there. I mean, I couldn't very well meet with you without counsel present."

He paused again, as if holding out some irresistible bait for Payne and the other cops. He seemed to wonder if their passion for solving mysteries might be used in his favor, if he could entice them—offer something in return for answers that only he could provide. He was, above all, a survivor.

Thinking of the five consecutive life terms he was facing with his confessions, Henkel waited for a response from Payne and the other detectives. A thin smile crossed his face. He carefully weighed each word: "But I would be honest with you. I don't know what anyone can offer me. I mean, I don't know what you can come up with."

Neither Payne nor any of the other lawmen in the room was as susceptible to suggestions as Glenn and Sasha Scott, Sue Dixon, Debbie Gentile.

Payne stared back at Henkel.

The interview was over.

And so was the career of a Pittsburgh version of Jack the Ripper, for the time being, anyway.

People do change. Ask any prison shrink.

# A Minister without Portfolio

By Abby Mendelson

It's snowing on Buena Vista Street, snowing all over the North Side. From his third-floor windows, children's writer Ken Sims has a commanding view of Downtown and Mount Washington. "My town," he beams. "A lot of people's town."

He also has a closeup view of boarded-up houses across the street, and is within earshot of fracases and street rumbles. The second time his house was broken into, Sims caught the intruder, who apologized, saying he didn't realize Sims was black, too. "Hey," Sims fumed, "that's *regardless*. You can't just Pontius Pilate it anymore. You can't just wash your hands. You have to be responsible. You have to say, 'yes, I *am* responsible.' "

Another time, Sims broke up a black-white fight around the corner. Believing his family had been insulted, a young black man had hurled a brick through a white man's window. Sims collared the youth. "That's not how we settle things," Sims told him. "You're not being a *man*."

"I'm not trying to save the world," Sims

explains. "Just a little part of it—the part that I live in."

There are more than flecks of gray in his thick, wavy hair, but Sims, 40, speaks in an earnest, youthful way. The fire still burns for education, for equality, colorblind equality. He recently helped a young neighbor get a scholarship to study agriculture—a white neighbor. Sims, for all practical purposes, is a minister without portfolio in his community.

His books are the high road he's taken to further those ends. *Captain Freedom*, a rousing, rhyming yarn about a slave-ship revolt, was published in 1978 and sold one hundred twenty-five thousand hardcover copies. It was such a strong effort that the *Captain Freedom* tour, as it was known, took Sims to Pitt, Clarion, and Indiana, and many public and parochial schools.

*The Voice*, poetry and photos about Martin Luther King, Jr., was a solid follow-up, pitched like *Captain Freedom*. (The city's School for the Performing Arts produced a stage version of it.)

For his third volume, Sims has reached farther down into childhood. *Araminta*, the real first name of underground railroad heroine Harriet Tubman, is a coloring book—a form that Sims is so taken with that he's recast his first two books this way as well.

Over the last twelve years, he's altered his

methods, from formal narrative to a more hands-on, family-oriented way to tell stories. He not only reformatted *Captain Freedom*, he rewrote it, extending the message of freedom and self-reliance to include ideas about the family and church. *The Voice*, dedicated to the late Ed Romano, a fellow KDKA cameraman, features simple statements about King's message, with repeated images of his face. "There's enough history about him," Sims says. "Hopefully parents will read this to their children, the kids will ask questions, and they'll talk to each other."

Never a man to sit still, Sims has other projects planned—a similar book on Nelson Mandela, the black South African leader recently freed from prison, and a series on heroes, including Lech Walesa, the Polish labor unionist and political leader.

Born in Jacksonville, raised in Baton Rouge, Sims moved to Pittsburgh in time to finish grammar school. With a master's degree in radio and TV, he's worked for fifteen years as a KDKA cameraman, a career that's taken him around the world. He's seen duty in Russia and China—and Italy, where he swapped books with the Pope, *Captain Freedom* for John Paul II's *The Jeweler's Shop*.

With a demanding day job, Sims is exacting but hardly a full-time writer. He does it nights and weekends at an antique desk on his third floor, and during daylight down-time. He produces as many as ten drafts for each book. "I get into great conflicts," he admits. "I don't want to lose the kids I want to reach. But I don't want to lose English. Because I'm appalled by black English. And rap scares me. Kids today are coming out unprepared. They can't talk. They can't read. They can't get a job. They can't even fill out an application. I want to *do* something about it. *Araminta* isn't *the* solution. But it's on the road to it."

A passage from *Araminta* sums up the Sims style and content:

> Blacks and whites working together
> Trying to stop slavery forever
> Different colors of skin
> Fighting slavery to win.

A good guess is that Sims will never make a great deal of money on his books—and not only because he insists on keeping the price to $1.50 or less. A classic soft touch, he is forever passing them out. He covers printing costs himself. One day, for example, he gave one hundred thirty copies of *The Voice* to nearby Martin Luther King School. He hopes to make enough profits to establish trade school as well as college scholarships.

"But knowing me," he says, "I'll get in a giving-away mood, and give half of them away."

There was a time, Sims admits, when he thought of leaving the city—when he'd fly to New York on weekends to work on media projects. But an odd thing happened. "I fell in love with Pittsburgh," he says. "It's a very personable town. You get to know people, and they're like family. You turn the corner—and it's right there.

"What good would it be for me to move to New York?" he asks. "I've got it here. It's an exciting time. The '90s is our decade—I can feel it. It's all of us getting together. . . . " He balls his hand into a fist.

"This is the wrong time to leave."

▲

# The Rox
# Candy Man

By Vince Leonard

Old Mike Sassano had one primary love—sports—and four secondary loves—his candy store, his radio, his parrot, and his trombone.

To two of them—the candy store and the radio—he was enslaved. He worked his candy store maybe fourteen hours a day, seven days a week. And every half hour, he listened to his radio.

He listened to Pie Traynor and Joe Tucker and Johnny Boyer for the scores, and to Gabriel Heatter and Edward R. Murrow and Lowell Thomas for the regular news. And he listened to Rosey Rowswell for the Pirates.

How he listened. Hunched up in his chair behind and to the right of his big showcase, he pressed his left ear to the arch-shaped talking box, its veneer cracked and peeling and showing thin layers of plywood, its round dial grimed beyond legibility.

He knew the stations by feel, by the switch of the dial. He had a sure touch that tuned in quickly to whatever station he wanted. He handled those knobs like a safecracker. Any time, you almost expected him to break out the sandpaper. Mike drank in the sounds.

If customers interrupted, Old Mike waited on them with one ear. Friends called—old-timers like The Mechanic and Santucci—and Mike would chat in his native tongue. On each and every half hour, Mike would end the conversation with an Italian parenthetical and an American closing, "Em beh, bye bye."

It was time for the scores and the news, and no idle talk could keep him from his rounds.

A screen door separated the store from Mike's personal quarters. He took his meals leaning away from the table so he could spot a customer. Someone once suggested installing a 75-cent bell above the front door to announce business. After the bell arrived, Mike still watched the door while balanced on two legs of the chair.

When little Jackie, about 5, came with a note for groceries, Mike had first crack at filling the order before his competitor saw the list.

Glasses hanging down on his long, bony nose, outstretched hands holding the note at a distance, Mike made mental check-offs of what he had in stock. When the list requested milk and pop and potato chips, Mike rustled them up from his meager provender.

For the rest—lunch meat and round steak—
he sent the young patron downstreet to
Dutch Karl's.

Sundays were bonanzas. Most other stores
were closed, but not Mike's. It was a sacri-
lege in those days, especially when you considered the location of his store, on Island
Avenue at McCoy Road in McKees Rocks,
just a stone's throw below Mother of Sorrows
Church.

For his festive Sunday sales day, Mike
shaved. The rest of the week he had ample
gray whiskers. And he appeared extra clean
on the Sabbath, much like a sheik who had
removed his desert mask. But the apparel
was always the same. He wore both belt and
suspenders to hold up baggy pants, made
baggier by the day's nickels, dimes, and
quarters in his pockets.

In rare moments of leisure, he struck a familiar pose—both hands inside both suspenders or both hands inside the belt. He
was lord of his domain.

Two windows, angling out above rickety,
blue-gray wood, were invitations to the
street, offering a peek at Mike's stock of
yoyos and whistles and workingman's gloves.

High on one window, the tea salesman had
stuck white block letters advertising his
product. On Mike's window, however, it read
S L A D A. The first A was missing but was

still outlined in the dried paste that had held
it there.

Inside was one counter of white marble,
an ice cream cabinet, pop machines, and his
main asset, the big showcase of sweets.
Perched in the middle was an oversized bird
cage housing Polly, whose "awwrk" and
"sonofabitch" and "bastard" always punctuated the deliveries of Rosey and Pie. Polly,
you see, was R-rated and Mike loved his pet
all the more for it.

On both news and sports broadcasts one
night, Mike heard of the shooting of Eddie
Waitkus, one-time Philadelphia first base-
man. For weeks after, this affected Mike's attitude toward life. Once, a bully broke up a
hopscotch game outside the store, next to the
weather-worn bench Mike provided for Sha-
fer bus riders to Kenmawr and Neville and
Coraopolis.

"They shoot men like Eddie Waitkus and
let that bully live," Mike said, almost without
rancor.

Another time, the same kid tried coaxing
Polly to swallow a ballbearing. "They shoot
men like Eddie Waitkus and Abe Lincoln
and let him live." Mike was angry.

On happy days, Mike broke out his trombone. He had healthy lungs, and the rich
sound wafted far and wide, down across
White Alley and Robinson and Page Streets,

past Bump Chiodo's leftover Victory Garden, across railroad tracks to the Bottoms and the banks of the Ohio River. A town legend was that Mike and his trombone once posed for a picture with John Philip Sousa.

Years wore on, and the trombone's range diminished. You could no longer hear it, say, in the Bottoms. Mike was nearly ninety when a foreboding sign appeared in the window, below the tea ad: "Olds Trombone for Sale," it read. Not very long after that Mike died.

There is just an empty lot now where he lived and worked.

Driving by and waiting for the red light to change, if you hunch up, close your eyes, and press an ear hard, the way Mike used to at his radio, you can still hear faint music coming from the Store of Dreams. You can hear, with a little imagination, the cuss words of Polly, and the scratchy voices of Rosey and Murrow, and that triumphant, mellow, trombone—and the change jingling in his baggy pants.

▲

Coming next from The ICONOCLAST PRESS:

**Pittsburgh Shysters,** a collection of crooked lawyers whose conduct was so unholy they were banished from the courtroom by their own colleagues;

**Pittsburgh Con Artists,** an anthology of swindlers whose brazen antics set them apart from common thieves.

To order additional copies of **Pittsburgh Characters,** send check or money order for $7.50 (Pennsylvanians add 6 percent sales tax) to:

The ICONOCLAST PRESS
PO Box 1826
Greensburg, PA 15601–6826